GRAMMAR
AND BEYOND 1A

Second Edition

with Academic Writing

Randi Reppen

CAMBRIDGE
UNIVERSITY PRESS

CAMBRIDGE
UNIVERSITY PRESS

University Printing House, Cambridge CB2 8BS, United Kingdom

One Liberty Plaza, 20th Floor, New York, NY 10006, USA

477 Williamstown Road, Port Melbourne, VIC 3207, Australia

314–321, 3rd Floor, Plot 3, Splendor Forum, Jasola District Centre, New Delhi – 110025, India

79 Anson Road, #06–04/06, Singapore 079906

Cambridge University Press is part of the University of Cambridge.

It furthers the University's mission by disseminating knowledge in the pursuit of education, learning and research at the highest international levels of excellence.

cambridge.org
Information on this title: cambridge.org/9781108784900

© Cambridge University Press 2021

First published 2013
Second edition 2021

20 19 18 17 16 15 14 13 12 11 10 9 8 7 6 5 4 3 2 1

Printed in Dubai by Oriental Press

A catalogue record for this publication is available from the British Library

ISBN Student's Book 1A with Online Practice 978-1-108-78490-0

Additional resources for this publication at www.cambridge.org/grammarandbeyond

About the Author

Randi Reppen is Professor of Applied Linguistics and TESL at Northern Arizona University (NAU) in Flagstaff, Arizona. She has over 20 years' experience teaching ESL students and training ESL teachers, including 11 years as the Director of NAU's Program in Intensive English. Randi's research interests focus on the use of corpora for language teaching and materials development. In addition to numerous academic articles and books, she is the author of *Using Corpora in the Language Classroom* and a co-author of *Basic Vocabulary in Use*, 2nd edition, both published by Cambridge University Press.

Corpus Consultants

Michael McCarthy is Emeritus Professor of Applied Linguistics at the University of Nottingham, UK, and Adjunct Professor of Applied Linguistics at Pennsylvania State University. He is a co-author of the corpus-informed *Touchstone* series and the award-winning *Cambridge Grammar of English*, both published by Cambridge University Press, among many other titles, and is known throughout the world as an expert on grammar, vocabulary, and corpus linguistics.

Jeanne McCarten has over 30 years of experience in ELT/ESL as a teacher, publisher, and author. She has been closely involved in the development of the spoken English sections of the *Cambridge International Corpus*. Now a freelance writer, she is co-author of the corpus-informed *Touchstone* series and *Grammar for Business*, both published by Cambridge University Press.

Advisory Panel

The ESL advisory panel has helped to guide the development of this series and provided invaluable information about the needs of ESL students and teachers in high schools, colleges, universities, and private language schools throughout North America.

Neta Simpkins Cahill, Skagit Valley College, Mount Vernon, WA

Shelly Hedstrom, Palm Beach State College, Lake Worth, FL

Richard Morasci, Foothill College, Los Altos Hills, CA

Stacey Russo, East Hampton High School, East Hampton, NY

Alice Savage, Lone Star College-North Harris, Houston, TX

Scope and Sequence

Avoid Common Mistakes	Academic Writing
Avoiding *be + no*; avoiding sentences beginning with *be*	**Thinking about Speaking and Writing** • Compare the skills • Add information in a chart
Remembering capital letters and punctuation; avoiding contractions with short answers to *yes/no* questions	**Writing about a Person** Writing prompt: *Write about someone in your family.* • Use pronouns to avoid repetition • Brainstorm
Remembering *a/an*; remembering subject/verb agreement	• Write simple sentences
Using *this/that and these/those*; using possessives	• Use *and* to add details • Revise and edit
Remembering where to put adjectives; avoiding plural adjectives	**Writing about a Place** Writing prompt: *Write about your country.* • Identify main ideas • Classify key words
Remembering *in*, *on*, and *at*	• Paragraph structure and topic sentences • Use prepositional phrases to write about places • Use an outline to organize ideas
Using *there is / there are*; avoiding contractions in academic writing	• Use *there is* and *there are* to introduce details • Write, revise, and edit paragraphs

Avoid Common Mistakes	Academic Writing
Avoiding *do/does* in negative statements with *be*; avoiding *be* with simple present verbs	**Writing about Daily Life** Writing prompt: *Write about the life of a classmate.* • Brainstorm
Remembering *Do/Does* in simple present questions with *have*; Avoiding *Do/Does* in questions with *be*	• Identify main ideas and details • Use a chart to organize details
Remembering *do/does*; avoiding *-s* with *he/she/it*	• Write a paragraph • Add details about time and place • Revise and edit
Remembering a comma with conjunctions; using conjunctions	**Writing Formal Emails** Writing prompt: *Write an email to a professor.* • Write a formal email
Remembering simple past verbs to talk about the past; remembering the base form of the verb after *did not / didn't*	**Narrative Paragraph** Writing prompt: *Write a paragraph about the history of a business.* • Use a timeline to put past events in order • Brainstorm and research
Remembering *did* + subject + base form of the verb; avoiding the past form in information questions	• Add details to main events • Use a paragraph planner to organize ideas
Using *was/were*; Remembering the correct form with *born*	• Use time-order transition signals • Write a narrative paragraph
Remembering the correct spelling of *when*, *before*, and *after*; Remembering the subject in the main clause and the time clause	• Use past time clauses • Revise and edit

Avoid Common Mistakes	Academic Writing
Avoiding *a / an* with noncount nouns; avoiding the plural with noncount nouns	**Descriptive Paragraphs** Writing prompt: *Write about popular food in your country.* • Use an idea map to brainstorm
Remembering *many* with plural nouns; remembering *any* with negative statements and *some* with affirmative statements	• Use an idea map to organize • Complete an outline • Use quantifiers to describe food
Avoiding *a/an* with noncount nouns; Avoiding *the* to talk about things or people in general	• Use articles in a paragraph • Write descriptive paragraphs
Avoiding the plural with possessive pronouns; remembering *any* + in negative statements	• Use collocations • Revise and edit
Avoiding *no* in negative imperatives; remembering an apostrophe in *don't*	**Expository Paragraph** Writing prompt: *Write a paragraph about someone who is a good role model to you. Explain why that person is a good role model.* • Balance facts and qualities • Brainstorm
Avoiding *-s* with *can* and *could*; remembering the base form with *can* and *could*	• Write concluding sentences • Use statements of ability • Organize ideas
Remembering the correct word order for making requests; remembering the base form of the verb after *can*, *could*, *may*, or *would*	• Use adjectives and adverbs to describe challenges • Write an expository paragraph • Revise and edit
Remembering *be* and verb + *-ing* for the present progressive	**Process Paragraph** Writing prompt: *Describe the Sydney Triathlon.* • Use a line diagram to think about steps in a process • Brainstorm
Remembering *was / were* + verb + *-ing* for the past progressive	• Use transition words to order events in a process • Describe a process diagram • Organize events

Avoid Common Mistakes	Academic Writing
Using subject and object pronouns; avoiding putting the pronoun before the noun	• Remove unrelated information from a paragraph • Write a process paragraph
Using infinitives and gerunds; Avoiding *wanna* in writing	• Use gerunds to add information • Revise and edit
Remembering the verb *be* in *be going to*; remembering *will* for predictions	**Opinion Paragraph** Writing prompt: *"The Internet wastes our time. It does not help us do more work."* Do you agree or disagree? • Recognize advantages and disadvantages. • Brainstorm advantages and disadvantages • What to do after brainstorming
Avoiding using *can* for predictions; avoiding using *can* for certainty	• Analyze a writing prompt/ question • Use a table to organize details • Write a topic sentence for an opinion paragraph
Using *should* and *ought*; avoiding putting *probably* after the *ought to*	• Use phrases to introduce opinions • Write an opinion paragraph
Avoiding *to* after *must*; avoiding *need to* for conclusions	• Connect ideas with *and*, *also*, and *too* • Revise and edit
Avoiding -*ly* in irregular adverbs; avoiding confusion with *good* and *well*; avoiding putting the adverb between a verb and its object	**Description and Opinion** Writing prompt: *Describe the place where you live now or where you are from. Write about its positive and negatives. Include your opinions.* • Use a T-chart to brainstorm positives and negatives
Avoiding *more* with *better* and *worse*; avoiding *that* and *then* after a comparative	• Use comparative adjectives to describe a place • Use a T-chart to take notes and organize ideas
Avoiding the comparative for more than two things; avoiding using *most* and -*est* together	• Use contrast words to signal a shift • Write a descriptive paragraph with opinion • Use superlative adjectives • Revise and edit

Introduction to *Grammar and Beyond*, 2nd edition

Grammar and Beyond is a research-based and content-rich grammar and academic writing series for beginning to advanced-level students. The series focuses on the most commonly used English grammar structures and practices all four skills in a variety of authentic and communicative contexts.

Grammar and Beyond is Research-Based

The grammar presented in this series is informed by years of research on the grammar of written and spoken English as it is used in college lectures, textbooks, academic essays, high school classrooms, and conversations between instructors and students. This research, and the analysis of over one billion words of authentic written and spoken language data known as the *Cambridge International Corpus*, has enabled the authors to:

- Present grammar rules that accurately represent how English is actually spoken and written

- Identify and teach differences between the grammar of written and spoken English

- Focus more attention on the structures that are commonly used, and less on those that are rarely used, in writing and speaking

- Help students avoid the most common mistakes that English language learners make

- Choose reading topics that will naturally elicit examples of the target grammar structure

- Introduce important vocabulary from the Academic Word List

Special Features of *Grammar and Beyond*

Realistic Grammar Presentations

Grammar is presented in clear and simple charts. The grammar points presented in these charts have been tested against real-world data from the *Cambridge International Corpus* to ensure that they are authentic representations of actual use of English.

Data from the Real World

Many of the grammar presentations and application sections include a feature called Data from the Real World. Concrete and useful points discovered through analysis of corpus data are presented and practiced in exercises that follow.

Avoid Common Mistakes

Every unit features an Avoid Common Mistakes section that develops students' awareness of the most common mistakes made by English language learners and gives them an opportunity to practice detecting and correcting these errors. This section helps students avoid these mistakes in their own work. The mistakes highlighted in this section are drawn from a body of authentic data on learner English known as the *Cambridge Learner Corpus*, a database of over 35 million words from student essays written by non-native speakers of English and information from experienced classroom teachers.

Academic Vocabulary

Every unit in *Grammar and Beyond* includes words from the Academic Word List (AWL), a research-based list of words and word families that appear with high frequency in English-language academic texts. These words are introduced in the opening text of the unit, recycled in the charts and exercises, and used to support the theme throughout the unit. By the time students finish each level, they will have been exposed several times to a carefully selected set of level-appropriate AWL words, as well as content words from a variety of academic disciplines.

Academic Writing

Every unit ends with an Academic Writing section. In Levels 1 through 3, this edition of *Grammar and Beyond* teaches students to write academically using writing cycles that span several units. Each writing cycle is organized around a writing prompt and focuses on a specific type of academic writing, such as descriptive, narrative, and process. Students move through the steps of the writing process - Brainstorm, Organize, Write, Edit - while learning and practicing new writing skills and ways to incorporate the unit grammar into their writing. In Level 4, the entire scope and sequence is organized around the types of essays students write in college, and focuses on the grammar rules, conventions, and structures needed to master them.

Series Levels

The following table provides a general idea of the difficulty of the material at each level of *Grammar and Beyond*. These are not meant to be interpreted as precise correlations.

	Description	TOEFL IBT	CEFR Levels
Level 1	Beginning	20 – 34	A1 – A2
Level 2	Low Intermediate to Intermediate	35 – 54	A2 – B1
Level 3	High Intermediate	55 – 74	B1 – B2
Level 4	Advanced	75 – 95	B2 – C1

Student Components

Student's Book with Online Practice

Each unit, based on a high-interest topic, teaches grammar points appropriate for each level in short, manageable cycles of presentation and practice. Academic Writing focuses on the structure of the academic essay in addition to the grammar rules, conventions, and structures that students need to master in order to be successful college writers. Students can access both the Digital Workbook and Writing Skills Interactive using their smartphones, tablets, or computers with a single log-in. See pages xviii–xxiii for a Tour of a Unit.

Digital Workbook

The Digital Workbook provides additional online exercises to help master each grammar point. Automatically-graded exercises give immediate feedback for activities such as correcting errors highlighted in the Avoid Common Mistakes section in the Student's Book. Self-Assessment sections at the end of each unit allow students to test their mastery of what they learned. Look for [ ] in the Student's Book to see when to use the Digital Workbook.

Writing Skills Interactive

Writing Skills Interactive is a self-grading course to practice discrete writing skills, reinforce vocabulary, and give students an opportunity with additional writing practice. Each unit has:

- Vocabulary review
- Short text to check understanding of the context
- Animated presentation of target unit writing skill
- Practice activities
- Unit Quiz to assess progress

Teacher Resources

A variety of downloadable resources are available on Cambridge One (cambridgeone.org) to assist instructors, including the following:

Teacher's Manual

- Suggestions for applying the target grammar to all four major skill areas, helping instructors facilitate dynamic and comprehensive grammar classes
- An answer key and audio script for the Student's Book
- Teaching tips, to help instructors plan their lessons
- Communicative activity worksheets to add more in-class speaking practice

Assessment

- Placement Test
- Ready-made, easy-to-score Unit Tests, Midterm, and Final in .pdf and .doc formats
- Answer Key

Presentation Plus

Presentation Plus allows teachers to digitally project the contents of the Student's Book in front of the class for a livelier, interactive classroom. It is a complete solution for teachers because it includes easy-to-access answer keys and audio at point of use.

Acknowledgements

The publisher and author would like to thank these reviewers and consultants for their insights and participation:

Marty Attiyeh, The College of DuPage, Glen Ellyn, IL

Shannon Bailey, Austin Community College, Austin, TX

Jamila Barton, North Seattle Community College, Seattle, WA

Kim Bayer, Hunter College IELI, New York, NY

Linda Berendsen, Oakton Community College, Skokie, IL

Anita Biber, Tarrant County College Northwest, Fort Worth, TX

Jane Breaux, Community College of Aurora, Aurora, CO

Anna Budzinski, San Antonio College, San Antonio, TX

Britta Burton, Mission College, Santa Clara, CA

Jean Carroll, Fresno City College, Fresno, CA

Chris Cashman, Oak Park High School and Elmwood Park High School, Chicago, IL

Annette M. Charron, Bakersfield College, Bakersfield, CA

Patrick Colabucci, ALI at San Diego State University, San Diego, CA

Lin Cui, Harper College, Palatine, IL

Jennifer Duclos, Boston University CELOP, Boston, MA

Joy Durighello, San Francisco City College, San Francisco, CA

Kathleen Flynn, Glendale Community College, Glendale, CA

Raquel Fundora, Miami Dade College, Miami, FL

Patricia Gillie, New Trier Township High School District, Winnetka, IL

Laurie Gluck, LaGuardia Community College, Long Island City, NY

Kathleen Golata, Galileo Academy of Science & Technology, San Francisco, CA

Ellen Goldman, Mission College, Santa Clara, CA

Ekaterina Goussakova, Seminole Community College, Sanford, FL

Marianne Grayston, Prince George's Community College, Largo, MD

Mary Greiss Shipley, Georgia Gwinnett College, Lawrenceville, GA

Sudeepa Gulati, Long Beach City College, Long Beach, CA

Nicole Hammond Carrasquel, University of Central Florida, Orlando, FL

Vicki Hendricks, Broward College, Fort Lauderdale, FL

Kelly Hernandez, Miami Dade College, Miami, FL

Ann Johnston, Tidewater Community College, Virginia Beach, VA

Julia Karet, Chaffey College, Claremont, CA

Jeanne Lachowski, English Language Institute, University of Utah, Salt Lake City, UT

Noga Laor, Rennert, New York, NY

Min Lu, Central Florida Community College, Ocala, FL

Michael Luchuk, Kaplan International Centers, New York, NY

Craig Machado, Norwalk Community College, Norwalk, CT

Denise Maduli-Williams, City College of San Francisco, San Francisco, CA

Diane Mahin, University of Miami, Coral Gables, FL

Melanie Majeski, Naugatuck Valley Community College, Waterbury, CT

Jeanne Malcolm, University of North Carolina at Charlotte, Charlotte, NC

Lourdes Marx, Palm Beach State College, Boca Raton, FL

Susan G. McFalls, Maryville College, Maryville, TN

Nancy McKay, Cuyahoga Community College, Cleveland, OH

Dominika McPartland, Long Island Business Institute, Flushing, NY

Amy Metcalf, UNR/Intensive English Language Center, University of Nevada, Reno, NV

Robert Miller, EF International Language School San Francisco – Mills, San Francisco, CA

Marcie Pachino, Jordan High School, Durham, NC

Myshie Pagel, El Paso Community College, El Paso, TX

Bernadette Pedagno, University of San Francisco, San Francisco, CA

Tam Q Pham, Dallas Theological Seminary, Fort Smith, AR

Mary Beth Pickett, GlobalLT, Rochester, MI

Maria Reamore, Baltimore City Public Schools, Baltimore, MD

Alison M. Rice, Hunter College IELI, New York, NY

Sydney Rice, Imperial Valley College, Imperial, CA

Kathleen Romstedt, Ohio State University, Columbus, OH

Alexandra Rowe, University of South Carolina, Columbia, SC

Irma Sanders, Baldwin Park Adult and Community Education, Baldwin Park, CA

Caren Shoup, Lone Star College – CyFair, Cypress, TX

Karen Sid, Mission College, Foothill College, De Anza College, Santa Clara, CA

Michelle Thomas, Miami Dade College, Miami, FL

Sharon Van Houte, Lorain County Community College, Elyria, OH

Margi Wald, UC Berkeley, Berkeley, CA

Walli Weitz, Riverside County Office of Ed., Indio, CA

Bart Weyand, University of Southern Maine, Portland, ME

Donna Weyrich, Columbus State Community College, Columbus, OH

Marilyn Whitehorse, Santa Barbara City College, Ojai, CA

Jessica Wilson, Rutgers University – Newark, Newark, NJ

Sue Wilson, San Jose City College, San Jose, CA

Margaret Wilster, Mid-Florida Tech, Orlando, FL

Anne York-Herjeczki, Santa Monica College, Santa Monica, CA

Hoda Zaki, Camden County College, Camden, NJ

We would also like to thank these teachers and programs for allowing us to visit:

Richard Appelbaum, Broward College, Fort Lauderdale, FL

Carmela Arnoldt, Glendale Community College, Glendale, AZ

JaNae Barrow, Desert Vista High School, Phoenix, AZ

Ted Christensen, Mesa Community College, Mesa, AZ

Richard Ciriello, Lower East Side Preparatory High School, New York, NY

Virginia Edwards, Chandler-Gilbert Community College, Chandler, AZ

Nusia Frankel, Miami Dade College, Miami, FL

Raquel Fundora, Miami Dade College, Miami, FL

Vicki Hendricks, Broward College, Fort Lauderdale, FL

Kelly Hernandez, Miami Dade College, Miami, FL

Stephen Johnson, Miami Dade College, Miami, FL

Barbara Jordan, Mesa Community College, Mesa, AZ

Nancy Kersten, GateWay Community College, Phoenix, AZ

Lewis Levine, Hostos Community College, Bronx, NY

John Liffiton, Scottsdale Community College, Scottsdale, AZ

Cheryl Lira-Layne, Gilbert Public School District, Gilbert, AZ

Mary Livingston, Arizona State University, Tempe, AZ

Elizabeth Macdonald, Thunderbird School of Global Management, Glendale, AZ

Terri Martinez, Mesa Community College, Mesa, AZ

Lourdes Marx, Palm Beach State College, Boca Raton, FL

Paul Kei Matsuda, Arizona State University, Tempe, AZ

David Miller, Glendale Community College, Glendale, AZ

Martha Polin, Lower East Side Preparatory High School, New York, NY

Patricia Pullenza, Mesa Community College, Mesa, AZ

Victoria Rasinskaya, Lower East Side Preparatory High School, New York, NY

Vanda Salls, Tempe Union High School District, Tempe, AZ

Kim Sanabria, Hostos Community College, Bronx, NY

Cynthia Schuemann, Miami Dade College, Miami, FL

Michelle Thomas, Miami Dade College, Miami, FL

Dongmei Zeng, Borough of Manhattan Community College, New York, NY

Tour of a Unit

ACADEMIC WRITING FOCUS

appears at the beginning of the unit.

GRAMMAR IN THE REAL WORLD

presents the unit's grammar in a realistic context using contemporary texts.

UNIT 16 — Count and Noncount Nouns

Eating Habits

1 Grammar in the Real World

ACADEMIC WRITING
Descriptive paragraphs

A Do you think your diet is healthy? Read the article from a health magazine. What kinds of food are part of a healthy diet?

B Comprehension Check Answer the questions. Use the article to help you.

1 How do colorful fruit and vegetables help your health?

2 Why is a little dark chocolate good for you?

3 What type of oil is good for you?

4 How much water is good to drink each day?

C Notice Find the sentences in the article, and complete them with a or an or Ø for no article.

1 When you turn on _____ television or read _____ newspaper, you often find _____ information about healthy eating.

2 _____ food and _____ health get a lot of attention in the news these days.

3 Maybe you think _____ fat is bad for you, but people need a little fat in their diet.

4 It is _____ challenge to change your diet, but even small changes can help you stay healthy and happy.

Look at the noun after each space. Which of the nouns are things you can count? Which are things you cannot count?

Count and Noncount Nouns

Food for Health

When you turn on a television or read a **newspaper**, you often find **information** about healthy eating. **Food** and **health** get a lot of **attention** in the **news** these **days**. Researchers seem to find new **things** about how our **diet** affects us every day.

Everyone knows it is important to eat **fruit** and **vegetables**. Did you know that eating **fruit** and **vegetables** with different colors is especially good for your **health**? Green, red, blue, and orange **fruit** and **vegetables** all have different **vitamins**[1] to help hydrate you, and they help prevent different **diseases**.

Did you know that dark **chocolate** is good for you, too? Research shows that a little **chocolate** helps your **heart** and your **mood**.[2]

How about **fat**?[3] Maybe you think **fat** is bad for you, but people need a little **fat** in their diet. One type of healthy **fat** is omega-3 **oil**.[4] It comes from **fish** and helps your **heart**, **skin**, and **brain** stay healthy. For **vegetarians** or non-fish eaters, many **seeds**[5] and **nuts** also contain omega-3 **oil**. Omega-3 **oil** comes in **pills**, too.

Finally, **water** is an important part of a healthy **diet**. Try to drink at least six **glasses** of **water** a day, and you don't need to buy it. In most places, tap **water** from the kitchen **faucet** is just fine and tastes great!

It is a **challenge** to change your **diet**, but even small **changes** can help you stay healthy and happy.

[1] **vitamin:** a natural substance in food that is important for good health
[2] **mood:** the way someone feels at a particular time
[3] **fat:** a substance in plants and animals, often used for cooking
[4] **omega-3 oil:** a kind of healthy fat
[5] **seed:** a small hard part of a plant from which new plants can grow

194

Eating Habits **195**

NOTICE ACTIVITIES

draw students' attention to the structure, guiding their own analysis of form, meaning, and use.

GRAMMAR PRESENTATION

begins with an overview that describes the grammar in an easy-to-understand summary.

GRAMMAR APPLICATION

keeps students engaged with a wide variety of exercises that introduce new and stimulating content.

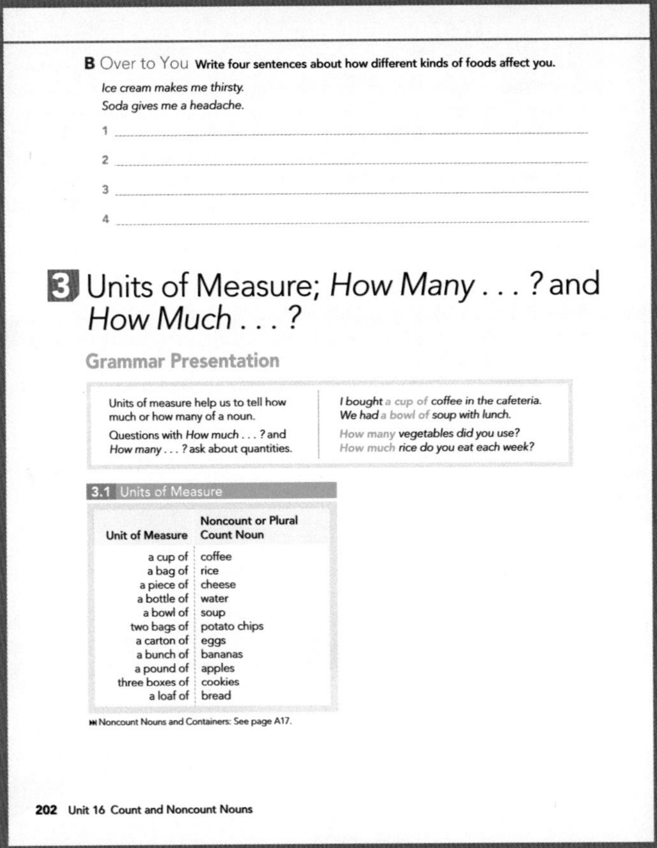

B Over to You **Write four sentences about how different kinds of foods affect you.**

Ice cream makes me thirsty.
Soda gives me a headache.

1 ______
2 ______
3 ______
4 ______

3 Units of Measure; *How Many . . . ?* and *How Much . . . ?*

Grammar Presentation

Units of measure help us to tell how much or how many of a noun.

Questions with *How much . . . ?* and *How many . . . ?* ask about quantities.

I bought a cup of coffee in the cafeteria.
We had a bowl of soup with lunch.

How many vegetables did you use?
How much rice do you eat each week?

3.1 Units of Measure

Unit of Measure	Noncount or Plural Count Noun
a cup of	coffee
a bag of	rice
a piece of	cheese
a bottle of	water
a bowl of	soup
two bags of	potato chips
a carton of	eggs
a bunch of	bananas
a pound of	apples
three boxes of	cookies
a loaf of	bread

Noncount Nouns and Containers: See page A17.

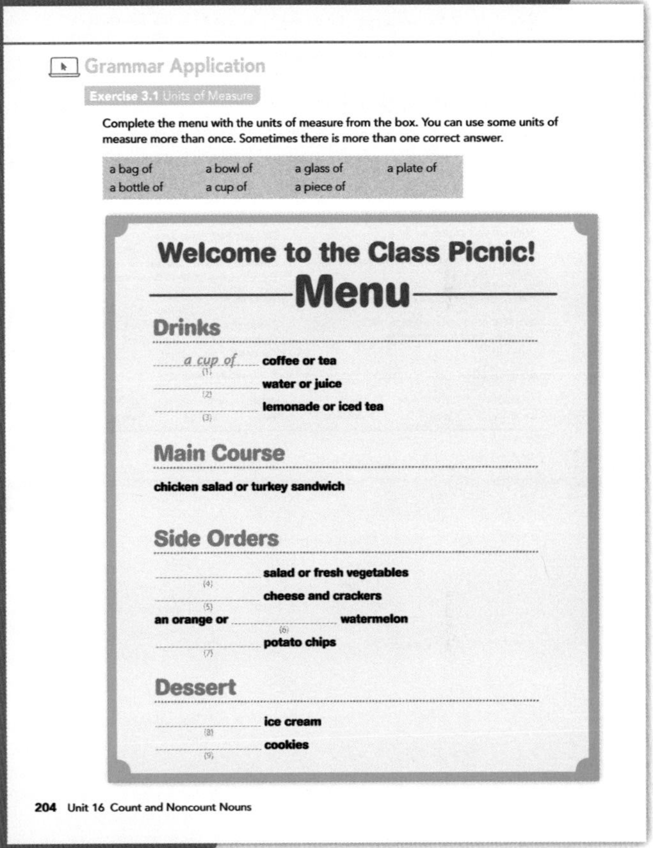

Grammar Application

Exercise 3.1 Units of Measure

Complete the menu with the units of measure from the box. You can use some units of measure more than once. Sometimes there is more than one correct answer.

a bag of	a bowl of	a glass of	a plate of
a bottle of	a cup of	a piece of	

Welcome to the Class Picnic!

Menu

Drinks

a cup of (1) **coffee or tea**
______ (2) **water or juice**
______ (3) **lemonade or iced tea**

Main Course

chicken salad or turkey sandwich

Side Orders

______ (4) **salad or fresh vegetables**
______ (5) **cheese and crackers**
an orange or ______ (6) **watermelon**
______ (7) **potato chips**

Dessert

______ (8) **ice cream**
______ (9) **cookies**

CHARTS

provide clear guidance on the form, meaning, and use of the target grammar for ease of instruction and reference.

THEME-RELATED EXERCISES

boost fluency by providing grammar practice in a variety of different contexts.

Exercise 3.2 *How Much . . . ? and How Many . . . ?*

A Complete each question about the class picnic with *How much* or *How many*.
Then listen to the conversation about the picnic and answer the questions.

1 _How many_ students are there in the class? _18_
2 _____ money do they have? _____
3 _____ people want water? _____
4 _____ juice do they need? _____
5 _____ people want sandwiches? _____
6 _____ bags of potato chips do they need? _____
7 _____ salad do they need? _____
8 _____ cheese do people want? _____
9 _____ people want an orange? _____
10 _____ watermelon do they need? _____

B Pair Work Plan a class picnic. Use the menu in Exercise 3.1 and the questions in A
to help you.
  A How many students are there in our group?
  B There are eight. How many people want water?

DATA FROM THE REAL WORLD

Research shows that these are some of the most common noncount nouns:

equipment	homework	love	music	traffic
fun	information	mail	peace	weather
furniture	insurance	money	software	work

Noncount nouns are the names of:

materials: oil, plastic, wood	*Oil* costs a lot these days.
groups of things: money, cash, furniture, jewelry	The *jewelry* in this store is expensive.
subjects: chemistry, geography, psychology	*Chemistry* doesn't interest me at all.
weather: snow, ice, fog	There's always *snow* in the winter here.

Some noncount nouns end in -s, but they take a singular verb:

subjects: economics, physics, politics	*Economics* was my best subject in high school.
activities: aerobics, gymnastics	*Gymnastics* is my favorite sport.
other: news	The *news* is really good.

Students often make mistakes with noncount nouns, especially these:

| information | equipment | advice | research | knowledge | furniture |
| behavior | work | homework | software | damage | training |

QR CODES

give easy access to audio at point of use.

CONTEXTUALIZED PRACTICE

moves from controlled to open-ended,
teaching meaningful language for real
communicative purposes.

DATA FROM THE REAL WORLD

takes students beyond traditional
information and teaches them how the
unit's grammar is used in authentic
situations, including differences between
spoken and written use.

HOW TO USE A QR CODE

1 Open the camera on your smartphone.

2 Point it at the QR code.

3 The camera will automatically scan the code.
   If not, press the button to take a picture.

* Not all cameras automatically scan QR codes.
  You may need to download a QR code reader.
  Search "QR free" and download an app.

Count and Noncount Nouns

4 Avoid Common Mistakes ⚠ 💻

1 **Do not use *a* / *an* with noncount nouns.**
I'm doing a research on eating habits.

2 **Do not make noncount nouns plural or use them with a plural verb.**
~~advice~~
My teacher gave me some useful ~~advices~~.

3 **Do not use *these* or *those* with noncount nouns.**
~~this information is~~
I hope these informations are useful.

4 **Use *how much* with noncount nouns, and use *how many* with count nouns.**
~~much~~   ~~many~~
How many money do you have?   How much classes did you take?

Editing Task

Find and correct the mistakes on this school's website.

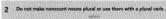

LaMoor College Student Advice Center
Hotel and Restaurant Program Frequently Asked Questions

1. Where can I get an information about the study program?
   Look on the department website for these informations. You can also find an important news on the website and lots of helpful information.
2. How much classes can I take each semester?
   Students can take four to six classes each semester.
3. Is there modern equipments at the college?
   Yes, our kitchens have brand-new equipment and furnitures.
4. How many homework do professors assign?
   Every class is different, but professors will always help you if you have a problem with your homeworks.
5. Does the school give an advice about employment and works?
   Yes! Our career counselor has knowledges about local employers.

AVOID COMMON MISTAKES

is based on a database of over 135,000 essays. Students learn to avoid the most common mistakes English language learners make and develop self-editing skills to improve their speaking and writing.

EDITING TASK

gives learners an opportunity to identify and correct commonly made errors and develop self-editing skills needed in their university studies.

ACADEMIC WRITING

concentrates on specific stages of the writing process: Brainstorm, Organize, Write, Edit.

REAL WORLD MODEL

incorporates the unit grammar into common types of writing for students to understand and analyze.

---

5 Academic Writing

Descriptive Paragraphs

Brainstorm › Organize › Write › Edit

In this writing cycle (Units 16–19), you are going to answer the prompt below. In this unit (16), you will look at an article about food and then brainstorm ideas for your writing.

Write about popular food in your country.

Exercise 5.1 Preparing to Write

Work with a partner. Ask and answer the questions. Then take turns describing the food.
1 What foods do you like from your country?
2 What foods do you like from other countries?
3 What foods do you like to eat in restaurants?

Exercise 5.2 Focusing on Vocabulary

Read the words in bold. Match the sentences to the pictures.
1 I eat **meat** for dinner. I like burgers or steak. _____
2 The restaurant always **serves** tea **with** a cookie. _____
3 I buy **vegetables** at the market in my city. _____
4 My dad is a fisherman, so we eat a lot of **fish**. _____
5 A popular **dish** for breakfast in the United States is pancakes. _____
6 In Mexico, beans and **rice** are popular. _____
7 My favorite **meal** of the day is breakfast. I have cereal and orange juice every morning. _____

a   b   c   d
e f   g

Count and Noncount Nouns

Popular Cuisines

Arab cuisine

1 At an Arab restaurant, you can find delicious **meat dishes**. Two popular types of dishes are *shawarma* and *kabsa*. Shawarma is a savory meat dish. The
5 meat is **served** in pita bread **with vegetables**. Kabsa is a popular **meal** in many Middle Eastern countries. Kabsa is a dish with **rice**, meat, and vegetables. There are many different ways to prepare kabsa. If you like meat dishes, you will
10 enjoy your meal at a Middle Eastern restaurant.

Australian cuisine

2 If you are in Australia, you must try a crocodile or kangaroo dish! Many Australian restaurants serve crocodile curry. Crocodile meat is tasty and very
15 good for you. (It is better if you eat crocodile than if a crocodile eats you!) Kangaroo meat is also good for you. Kangaroo burgers are served on a type of bread. Australian restaurants also serve many great fish dishes.

20 **Cambodian cuisine**

3 At a Cambodian restaurant, there are many types of dishes. Cambodians like **fish** with rice. Cambodian dishes are served with a lot of vegetables. They are very popular in Cambodian
25 cuisine. One famous dish is *amok trey*. Cambodians prepare amok trey with fish, nuts, coconut milk, and eggs. There are many tasty dishes, but this is one of the best.

Eating Habits **209**

LEARNER OUTCOMES

are mapped out at the beginning of each writing cycle and section.

MY WRITING

helps students develop their academic writing
at various stages of the writing process.

Count and Noncount Nouns

Exercise 5.3 Comprehension Check

Read the text on page 209. Answer the questions.

1 Where is *kabsa* a very popular dish? _____

2 Which dishes are served in or on bread? _____

3 Which kinds of meat are good for you? _____

4 How many cuisines have rice dishes? Name them. _____

5 How many cuisines have fish dishes? Name them. _____

Exercise 5.4 Noticing the Grammar and Structure

Work with a partner. Complete the tasks.

1 Circle four examples of the article *a* in paragraph 1. Is the noun after each example count or non-count?

2 Underline the non-count nouns in paragraph 3.

3 What tense are the verbs in the text? Why does the writer use this tense?

4 Who is the writer's audience: college students, tourists, or chefs?

Using an Idea Map

An **idea map**, or **mind map**, is a diagram for brainstorming and
organizing information. A good way to use an idea map is to write
down all the words and ideas about a topic that you can think of. Then
look for connections between those words and ideas.

Exercise 5.5 Applying the Skill

Work with a partner. Follow the steps to complete the idea map on page 211.

1 Look at paragraph 1 on page 209. Write the words that describe shawarma in the box. Add
any other words and ideas that you know about the dish or Middle Eastern food.

2 Think of connections between these words and ideas. Use the questions to help you.

* What is it made of?

* What does it taste like?

* What is it served with?

3 Write the connected words and ideas in one of the circles in the idea map below.

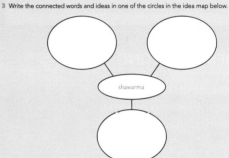

My Writing

Exercise 5.6 Brainstorming

Work in groups of 2 or 3 students. If possible, work with classmates from different countries.

1 Brainstorm at least three popular dishes from your country.
_____ _____ _____

2 Describe each dish. Use the questions to help you.

* What is it made of?

* What does it taste like?

* What is it served with?

* When do people eat it?

* Do you like it? Why or why not?

3 Write three sentences about food from your country. Use count and non-count nouns correctly.
_____
_____
_____
_____

Kahoot!

for Grammar and Beyond
cambridge.org/kahoot/grammarandbeyond

What is Kahoot!?
Kahoot! is a game-based learning platform that makes it easy to create, share and play fun learning games and trivia quizzes in minutes. You can play Kahoot! on any mobile device or laptop with an internet connection.

What can you use kahoots for?
Kahoots can be used for review, formative assessment or homework.

When should you play Kahoot?
You can play kahoot quizzes before starting the unit as a diagnostic, during the unit as formative assessment, or at the end of a unit to test student knowledge.

To launch a live game in the classroom, find the kahoot for the level and unit and simply click on "play".

Quiz Your English app

Quiz Your English is a fun new way to practice, improve, and test your English by competing against learners from all around the world. Learn English grammar with friends, discover new English words, and test yourself in a truly global environment.

- Learn to avoid common mistakes with a special section just for *Grammar and Beyond* users
- Challenge your friends and players wherever they are
- Watch where you are on the leaderboards

Statements with Present of *Be*

Tell Me about Yourself

1 Grammar in the Real World

A How do you introduce yourself to your instructors? What information do you give? Read the conversation between an adviser and a student. What are two interesting facts about Tomasz?

B Comprehension Check Circle the correct words.

1 Ms. Kim is **a student / an adviser**.

2 Tomasz is from **Poland / the United States**.

3 Tomasz is a salesclerk in his uncle's **store / restaurant**.

C Notice Complete the sentences. Use the conversation to help you.

1 I _____ Tomasz. Sorry I _____ late.

2 My major _____ computer science.

3 My brother and I _____ salesclerks. We _____ really interested in his business.

FIRST MEETING
WITH AN ADVISER

Tomasz	Hello, Ms. Kim. I'**m** Tomasz. Sorry I'**m** late for our meeting.
Ms. Kim	That's OK. Nice to meet you, Tomasz. Please have a seat.
Tomasz	Thanks.
Ms. Kim	First, I'**m** glad that you'**re** here. As your adviser, I'**m** here to help you. I can help you
5	choose your classes, and I can help you with any problems.
Tomasz	Thanks, I need your help. I have a lot of questions about courses, instructors, and
	my program.
Ms. Kim	Good! But first I'd like to know more about you. Tell me about yourself.
Tomasz	Sure. I'**m** 19, and I'**m** a graduate of Central High School. I'**m** from Poland originally.
10 **Ms. Kim**	I see. What **are** some of your interests?
Tomasz	Well, I'**m** interested in cars and music. And I really like computers. My major **is**
	computer science.
Ms. Kim	Great. You know, the college has a lot of clubs. It'**s** a good way to meet people and
	practice English.
15 **Tomasz**	Well, I'**m** pretty busy most of the time. My brother and I **are** salesclerks in my uncle's store.
	We'**re** really interested in his business. I don't have much free time.
Ms. Kim	OK. I understand. Now, let's talk about your academic plans . . .

2 Present of *Be*: Affirmative Statements

Grammar Presentation

Be links ideas.	I 'm a student .

2.1 Full Forms (with Subject Pronouns)

SINGULAR

Subject	*Be*	
I	am	
You	are	late.
He She It	is	difficult.

PLURAL

Subject	*Be*	
We You They	are	from Seoul.

▶▶ Capitalization and Punctuation Rules: See page A1.

2.2 Contractions (with Nouns and Subject Pronouns)

SINGULAR	PLURAL
I am → I**'m** You are → You**'re** He is → He**'s** Tomasz is → Tomasz**'s** She is → She**'s** His mother is → His mother**'s** It is → It**'s** My name is → My name**'s**	We are → We**'re** You are → You**'re** They are → They**'re**

2.3 Using Present of *Be*

A The verb *be* "links" ideas. You can use *be* to link nouns or pronouns with words that give information about them.	*Tomasz is a student.* *They are from California.*
B Use the full forms of *be* in academic writing.	*I **am** a computer science major.* *I **am** in your grammar class.*

2.3 Using Present of *Be* (continued)

C Use contractions of *be* in conversation and informal writing.	*I'm* Ms. Kim. *They're* sick today.
D You can use *be* + noun • to talk about occupations.	*He's* a teacher. *They're* students.
• to identify things.	*It's* an English class. *My hobbies are* baseball and music. *My major is* math.
E You can use *be* + number to talk about ages.	*My sister is* 18. *His parents are* 49 years old.
F You can use *be* + adjective • to talk about nationalities.	*I'm* Canadian. *His parents are* South Korean.
• to describe people and things.	*Jun-Ho is* tall. *My sister is* sick. *Our reading class is* interesting.
G You can use *be* + preposition • to talk about hometowns and places.	*My parents are* from Seoul. *I'm* from California.
• to talk about where people and things are.	*She is* at home. *We are* in Los Angeles.
• to talk about the groups, such as teams or clubs, that people are in.	*My friends and I are* in a band. *He is* on the basketball team.

Grammar Application

Exercise 2.1 Present of *Be*: Full Forms

A Complete the sentences about a student, using *am*, *is*, and *are*.

1 My name is Ling. I ___*am*___ a student at the University of Florida.

2 My friend Ana and I _____ in Science 101.

3 Mr. Johnson _____ a good instructor.

4 The class _____ interesting.

5 My classmates _____ crazy about science.

6 Ana _____ smart.

7 Ana and I _____ seniors this year.

B Look at the underlined word(s). Circle the subject pronoun that replaces the underlined words.

1 <u>My college</u> is in Detroit, Michigan. **It / She** is a good school.

2 <u>Jorge and Lisa</u> are in Grammar 110. **They / We** are in a fun class.

3 <u>Mrs. Chapple</u> is a great teacher. **It / She** is also very nice.

4 <u>Marcos</u> is crazy about grammar. **He / They** is never late for class.

5 <u>My brother</u> is smart. **He / It** is an excellent student.

6 <u>My mother</u> is a nurse. **She / It** is always very busy.

7 <u>My sister</u> and I are sick. **She / We** are at home today.

C Complete the student's online profile. Use the full forms of *be* (*am, is, are*).

My name __*is*__ Cindy Wang. I _____ from
        (1)   (2)
Jackson, Illinois. My parents _____ from China
                              (3)
originally. I _____ 20 years old. I _____ now
             (4)   (5)
a student at the University of Texas. My major _____
                                              (6)
public health. My favorite subjects _____ math and
                                    (7)
biology. I _____ interested in sports and drawing.
          (8)
My friend Bev and I _____ servers in a restaurant on
                    (9)
weekends. My sister _____ still a high school student
                    (10)
in Illinois.

D Over to You Complete the sentences with the correct full form of *be* and the information about you. Then read your sentences to your partner. How many of your sentences are the same?

1 My name _____ _____ .
            (be)   (name)

2 I _____ from _____ .
     (be)   (country)

3 I _____ _____ .
     (be)   (age)

4 My major _____ _____ .
              (be)   (subject)

5 My favorite class _____ _____ .
                       (be)   (name of class)

6 I _____ interested in _____ .
     (be)   (name of things)

7 I _____ .
   (Tell one more thing about yourself. Remember to use *be*.)

Exercise 2.2 Present of *Be*: Contractions

A Complete the sentences with *'m*, *'s*, or *'re*.

1 Ana   Hi, I ___'m___ Ana.
                  (1)

   Ron   Hi, Ana. My name _____ Ron. Nice to meet you.
                                (2)

   Ana   It _____ nice to meet you, too.
                (3)

   Ron   I _____ in Ms. Cook's class.
             (4)

   Ana   She _____ my teacher, too.
                 (5)
          You _____ in my class.
                 (6)

   Ron   Great. I think we _____ in Room 9.
                             (7)

2 Sara   Excuse me. I'm lost. My teacher _____ Mr. Martinez.
                                           (8)

   Ron   Mr. Martinez? He _____ in Room 10.
                           (9)

   Ana   Room 10 _____ over there. On the right.
                   (10)

   Sara   Oh, thanks.

   Ana   You _____ welcome.
                (11)

3 Ana   Ron, this is my friend Cathy. We _____ friends
                                            (12)
          from high school.

   Ron   Hi, Cathy.

   Cathy Hi, Ron!

   Ana   Cathy _____ on the basketball team.
                 (13)
          She _____ a great player.
                (14)

   Ron   Really? I _____ a big basketball fan.
                     (15)

   Ana   Well, come to our next game. It _____ on Friday.
                                          (16)

B Pair Work Introduce yourself to your partner. Use contractions. Then introduce your partner to a classmate.

Hi, I'm Alex. This is Hong-yin. He's from Texas. He's on the soccer team.

3 Present of *Be*: Negative Statements

Grammar Presentation

3.1 Full Forms

SINGULAR		
Subject	***Be + Not***	
I	**am not**	
You	**are not**	in class.
He She It	**is not**	

PLURAL		
Subject	***Be + Not***	
We You They	**are not**	students.

3.2 Negative Contractions

SINGULAR	PLURAL
I am not → I**'m not** You are not → You**'re not** / You **aren't** He is not → He**'s not** / He **isn't** She is not → She**'s not** / She **isn't** It is not → It**'s not** / It **isn't**	We are not → We**'re not** / We **aren't** You are not → You**'re not** / You **aren't** They are not → They**'re not** / They **aren't**

🌐 **DATA FROM THE REAL WORLD**

In conversation, people usually use **'s not** and **'re not** after pronouns.	He**'s not** 21. She**'s not** in class. They**'re not** here.
They usually use **isn't** and **aren't** after names and nouns.	Carlos **isn't** 21. Louise **isn't** in class. The boys **aren't** here.

🖱 Grammar Application

Exercise 3.1 Present of *Be*: Negative Statements with Full Forms

A Complete the sentences. Use *am not*, *is not*, or *are not*.

1 My roommate and I _____*are not*_____ math majors.

2 My friends _____ in my business class.

3 My cousin _____ married.

4 You _____ late.

5 My friend _____ in the library.

6 I _____ interested in chemistry.

7 Our instructor _____ from the United States.

8 The students _____ interested in history.

B Over to You **Write six negative sentences about yourself. Use the full form of *be*.**

1 I _*am not*_ a teacher.

2 I _____ from _____ .

3 I _____ interested in _____ .

4 I _____ a/an _____ major.

5 I _____ a/an _____ .

6 I _____ in _____ .

C Pair Work **Read your sentences to a partner. Are any of your sentences the same?**

Exercise 3.2 Affirmative or Negative?

A Read the online profiles. Complete the sentences with the correct affirmative or negative form of *be*. Use contractions when possible.

ONLINE PROFILES

	Yoko Akeda	Luiz da Costa
Age	21	35
Hometown	Los Angeles, California	New York, New York
Occupation or job; location	student at Glen College	instructor at Glen College
Interested in . . .	music, art museums	music, biking
Not interested in . . .	cooking, computer games	movies, cooking

1 Yoko _*is*_ 21. She _*'s not*_ 35.

2 Yoko and Luiz _____ the same age.

3 Luiz _____ an instructor.
He _____ a student.

4 Yoko _____ from New York. She
_____ from Los Angeles.

5 Luiz _____ from New York. He _____
from Los Angeles.

6 They _____ interested in music.
They _____ interested in cooking.

7 Luiz _____ interested in movies.

B Listen. Where are these people? Complete the sentences with the correct pronouns and forms of *be*. Use contractions when possible.

at home

at work

in class

at the movies

at the doctor's office

at the stadium

1 Carlos is sick. ____*He's*____ at the doctor's office. ___*He's not*___ at work.

2 Ana and her boss _____ in class. _____ in the office.

3 Juan and his children _____ at the doctor's office. _____ at home.

4 Karen is with her classmates and her teacher. _____ in class.
_____ at the stadium.

5 David is a big baseball fan. _____ at the stadium. _____ at home.

6 Ling and John are interested in movies. _____ at Drew's apartment.
_____ at the movies.

C Pair Work Tell a partner about four people you know. Where are they today?

My brother is at work. He's a salesclerk in a store . . .

Exercise 3.3 Negative of *Be*

Complete the conversations. Use *'s not* and *'re not* after pronouns and *isn't* and *aren't* after names and nouns.

1 **Sara** Hello. Accounting Department.

Ben Louise?

Sara No, it's Sara. Louise __*isn't*__ here.

(1)
She _____ at work today.

(2)

2 **Sam** Oh, no! My wallet _____ in my bag! It's on
the bus! (3)

   Man No, it _____ on the bus. Look, here it is. (4)

3 **Lara** Where are your brothers? The game's on TV, and
they _____ here. (5)

   Joe They _____ interested in baseball. They _____ (6) (7)
interested in sports.

4 Avoid Common Mistakes ⚠

1 **Use *be* to link ideas.**
      is
    He∧an engineering student.

2 **Use *be* + *not* to form negative statements with *be*. Do not use *be* + *no*.**
      not
    Ana is no a science teacher.

3 **A statement has a subject. Do not begin a statement with *be*.**
    She is
    Is my sister's best friend.

Editing Task

Correct nine more mistakes. Rewrite the sentences.

1 This my friend. *This is my friend.* _____

2 Her name Amy. _____

3 Amy and I roommates. _____

4 She 27. _____

5 She is no a student. _____

6 Is a science teacher. _____

7 Is very nice and very smart. _____

8 Amy is no in school today. _____

9 She sick. _____

10 Is at home. _____

5 Academic Writing

Thinking about Speaking and Writing

In this unit (1), you are going to think about the differences between speaking and writing.

Exercise 5.1 Noticing the Differences

Work with a partner. Look at the photos. How are speaking and writing different?
Write three ways.

1 _____

2 _____

3 _____

Exercise 5.2 Brainstorming and Organizing Ideas

Complete the tasks.

1 What do you talk about? What do you write? Make notes in the chart.

Things I talk about	Things I write
my sister	*homework*

2 Compare your answers with a partner's. Add any new information to your chart.

Read the conversation and paragraph. Then complete the exercises that follow.

Conversation	Paragraph
Luiz: Hi! I'm at school. Are you here too? Yuko: Uh, no, I'm at home. Luiz: At home? Yuko: Yeah. Luiz: Why? Yuko: Cuz I'm sick. Luiz: Oh, no! I hope you feel better soon. Yuko: Thanks. Luiz: You gonna go to class? Yuko: No. Luiz: OK, see you when you're better. Yuko: OK, bye.	My sister is a teacher. She works at a school and teaches math. She is a good teacher. My family is very happy that she is a teacher. We are proud of her.

Exercise 5.3 Noticing the Grammar

Work with a partner. Complete the tasks below.

1 Underline the verb *be* in the conversation and the paragraph.

2 Highlight the incomplete sentences.

3 Circle the contractions.

4 Double underline the informal words or expressions.

Exercise 5.4 Comparing the Skills

Write three differences between the conversation and the paragraph. Then compare your answers with your partner's.

1 _____

2 _____

3 _____

Exercise 5.5 Adding Information

Work with a partner. Complete the chart on a separate sheet of paper.

1 Write two more differences between speaking and writing in the chart.

When we speak …	When we write …

2 Compare your answers with another student pair. Add any new information to your chart.

1 Grammar in the Real World

A What is your class schedule? Read and listen to the conversations. Are Yuko's and Juan's classes the same?

B Comprehension Check **Read the sentences. Circle *True* or *False*.**

ACADEMIC WRITING

Writing about a person

Conversation A

1 Yuko and Juan are in Building H now.　　　True　　False

2 They are late for class.　　　True　　False

Conversation B

3 Mr. Walters is Yuko's grammar teacher.　　　True　　False

4 Computer lab is over at 4:15.　　　True　　False

C Notice **Find the questions in the conversations. Complete the questions.**

1 _____ you in my class?

2 _____ your class in Building H?

3 _____ that unusual?

4 _____ you sure?

Which words are at the beginning of the questions?

YUKO AND JUAN

CONVERSATION A (MONDAY)

 So, **is your next class writing?**

No, it's reading.

 Really? My next class is reading, too. **Are you in my class?** It's at 1:30.

5

Maybe. **Is your class in Building H?**

 Yes, it's in Building H, Room 308.

Then I'm in your class, too!

10

 Hmm. **Where's Building H?**

It's on the hill, over there.

 Oh, OK. **What time is it?**

It's 1:20. Uh-oh. We're late!

15 No, we aren't.

Are you sure?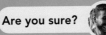

 Yes. Class is at 1:30.

Oh, you're right. That's good. Let's go.

CONVERSATION B (THURSDAY)

20 Hey, Juan. **How are you?**

I'm OK. **How are you?**

 I'm fine, thanks.

How are your classes?

 They're fine, but they're all really big.

25

Really? **How many students are in your classes?**

 About 25 to 30. **Is that unusual?**

No, it isn't. **Who's your grammar teacher?**

30

 Mr. Walters. He's funny, but his class is difficult.

So, **when's your next class?**

35

 Let me see. Today's Thursday. Computer lab is at 3:00.

When is it over?

 At 4:15. Let's meet after that.

40

2 Yes / No Questions and Short Answers with *Be*

Grammar Presentation

A *Yes / No* question is a question you can answer with *Yes* or *No*.	*"Is Yuko's class in Building H?"* *"Yes, it is." / "No, it isn't."*

2.1 Singular *Yes / No* Questions

Be	Subject	
Am	I	
Are	you	in class?
Is	he / she / it	

2.2 Singular Short Answers

AFFIRMATIVE

	Subject	Be
	I	**am.**
Yes,	you	**are.**
	he / she / it	**is.**

NEGATIVE

	Subject	Be + Not
	I	**am not.**
No,	you	**are not.**
	he / she / it	**is not.**

2.3 Plural *Yes / No* Questions

Be	Subject	
Are	we you they	late?

2.4 Plural Short Answers

AFFIRMATIVE

	Subject	Be
Yes,	we you they	**are.**

NEGATIVE

	Subject	Be + Not
No,	we you they	**are not.**

2.5 Negative Short Answers: Contractions

SINGULAR

No, I am not. → No, I**'m not**.

No, you are not. → No, you**'re not**.
No, you **aren't**.

No, he is not. → No, he**'s not**.
No, he **isn't**.

No, she is not. → No, she**'s not**.
No, she **isn't**.

No, it is not. → No, it**'s not**.
No, it **isn't**.

PLURAL

No, we are not. → No, we**'re not**.
No, we **aren't**.

No, you are not. → No, you**'re not**.
No, you **aren't**.

No, they are not. → No, they**'re not**.
No, they **aren't**.

2.6 Using *Yes / No* Questions and Short Answers with *Be*

A Use a question mark (?) at the end of questions.	*Is reading class hard?*	
B Put the verb *be* before the subject in *Yes / No* questions.	STATEMENT *YES / NO* QUESTION	SUBJECT VERB *Reading class is at 1:30.* *Is reading class at 1:30?*
C Use pronouns in short answers.	*"Is reading class hard?"* *"Yes, it is."*	
D Do not use contractions in short answers with *yes*.	*"Is class at 1:30?"* *"Yes, it is."* NOT *"Yes, it's."*	
E Use contractions in short answers with *no*.	*"Is Yuko late?"* *"No, she's not."* OR *"No, she isn't."*	
F Say *I don't know, I think so,* or *I don't think so* when you don't know or are not sure of the answer. Say *I don't know* when you don't know the answer. *I think so* means "maybe yes." *I don't think so* means "maybe no."	*"Is the library closed?"* *"I don't know."* OR *"I think so."* OR *"I don't think so."*	

A Circle the correct verbs to make questions. Then complete the answers with the correct pronoun and form of *be*. Use contractions when possible.

1 **(Is)/Are** your writing class in the morning?   Yes, __*it is*__ .

2 **Am/Are** you free on Fridays after lunch?   No, _____ .

3 **Are/Is** you always on time?   Yes, _____ .

4 **Is/Are** your teacher busy today?   Yes, _____ .

5 **Is/Are** you interested in sports?   No, _____ .

6 **Are/Is** your roommate in your class?   No, _____ .

7 **Is/Am** this an English class?   Yes, _____ .

8 **Is/Are** your next class in this building?   No, _____ .

B Write two questions and two answers about each picture. Use the words in parentheses.

1 a (late) _Is she late?_ _____   _Yes, she is._ _____

  b (at home) _____   _____

2 a (hungry) _____   _____

  b (at the store) _____   _____

3 a (open) _____   _____

  b (a white building) _____   _____

Exercise 2.2 Plural *Yes / No* Questions and Answers

Complete the conversation between two students, John and Eric. Then practice their conversation with a partner.

John (your teachers / friendly) *Are your teachers friendly?*
Eric (yes) *Yes, they are.*
John (you and your classmates / happy) _____
Eric (yes) _____
John (the homework assignments / easy) _____
Eric (no) _____
John (your classmates / on time) _____
Eric (no) _____
John (you and your friends / busy) _____
Eric (yes) _____
John (the exams / difficult) _____
Eric (yes) _____

Exercise 2.3 Singular and Plural *Yes / No* Questions and Answers

Read the paragraph from Julio's essay. Then write questions and answers about it. Use full forms of *be*.

Julio and Paulo

My roommate and I are in the English program at our college. Paulo is from Brazil, and I am from Venezuela. Paulo is a very good student, and he is very smart. I am a good student, but I am a little lazy. My classes are on Mondays, Wednesdays, and Fridays. Paulo's classes are every day from Monday to Friday. We are always busy, but on the weekend we relax.

1 Paulo and Julio / college students
   Are Paulo and Julio college students? Yes, they are.

2 they / from the same country
   _____

3 they / good students
   _____

4 Paulo / smart
   _____

5 Paulo / lazy
   _____

6 Julio's classes / every day from Monday to Friday
   _____

3 Information Questions with *Be*

Grammar Presentation

Use the question words *who, what, when, where,* and *how* to ask for information.	*What's your name?* *Who is the teacher?* *Where are the classrooms?*

3.1 Information Questions

SINGULAR SUBJECTS

Wh- Word	*Be*	Subject
Who		your teacher?
What		your major?
When	**is**	our exam?
Where		the building?
How		your class?

PLURAL SUBJECTS

Wh- Word	*Be*	Subject
Who		your teachers?
What		your plans?
When	**are**	your exams?
Where		your books?
How		your classes?

3.2 Contractions with Singular Subjects

Who is	→	**Who's**
What is	→	**What's**
When is	→	**When's**
Where is	→	**Where's**
How is	→	**How's**

3.3 Using Information Questions with *Be*

A Put a question mark (?) at the end of information questions.	*Who are those students?*
B Put the question word first in an information question.	*What is your name?*
C Answer information questions with information. Don't answer with *Yes* or *No*.	*"When is grammar class?"* *"At 10:00."*
D In conversations, most answers are not complete sentences. They are short answers.	*"Who's your teacher?"* *"Mr. Jones."*
E Note that with singular subjects it is common to use the contracted form of *is* with the question word.	*What's your name?* *Where's your class?*

3.4 Using *Wh-* Words with *Be*

A Use *who* to ask about people.	*Who's* our teacher? *Who* are your friends?	Ms. Williams. Marie and Elsa.
B Use *what* to ask about things.	*What* are your favorite classes? *What's* your phone number?	Grammar and writing. It's 368-555-9823.
C Use *where* to ask about places.	*Where's* your class? *Where* are you from? *Where* are your friends?	It's in Building H. Brazil. They're in the computer lab.
D Use *when* to ask about days or times.	*When's* your exam? *When* is lunch? *When* are our exams?	It's February 14. At noon. Next week.
E Use *how* to ask about health or opinions.	*How's* your mother? *How's* school?	She's well. Great!
F Use *how much* to ask about cost and amount. Use *how many* to ask about numbers. Use *how old* to ask about age.	*How much* is the movie? *How many* students are here? *How old* are your brothers?	Twenty dollars. Twelve. They're 17 and 15.

Grammar Application

Exercise 3.1 Information Questions with *Be*

A Complete the conversation between Joe and his mother. Use the correct *Wh-* word. Use contractions of *be*.

Mother	___*What's*___ your roommate's name? (1)
Joe	Mike.
Mother	_____ he from? (2)
Joe	Chicago.
Mother	_____ his major? (3)
Joe	I don't know. Mom, my history class is in five minutes.
Mother	_____ your instructor? (4)
Joe	I don't know his name. It's the first class.
Mother	_____ your class over? (5)
Joe	At 4:30. Please don't call before that.

B Complete the questions with *How, How much, How many,* or *How old.* Use the correct form of *be.*

1 _How are_ you?   I'm fine, thanks.

2 _____ you?   I'm 23.

3 _____ the textbook?   It's $86.

4 _____ students _____ in your English class?   Thirty.

5 _____ the sandwiches?   They're $12.95.

Exercise 3.2 Information Questions and Answers

Write questions about the tuition bill. Then write answers in complete sentences.

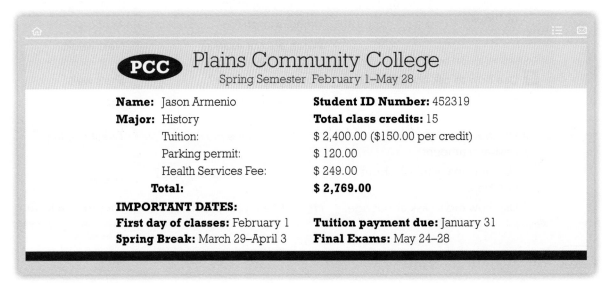

1 (What / the college's name) _What is the college's name? It's Plains Community College._

2 (What / the student's name) _____

3 (When / the spring semester) _____

4 (What / his major) _____

5 (How much / the tuition) _____

6 (How much / the parking permit) _____

7 (What / the total) _____

8 (When / final exams) _____

Exercise 3.3 More Information Questions and Answers

Pair Work With a partner, write five questions to ask your classmates. Ask questions about their classes, schedules, and school. Then interview your classmates. Write their answers in the chart.

Interview Questions	Your Classmates' Answers
1 *When are your classes?*	*My classes are on Monday and Wednesday.*
2	
3	
4	
5	
6	

4 Avoid Common Mistakes ⚠

1 **Begin a question with a capital letter. End with a question mark.**
W   ?
~~w~~here is Karla~~.~~

2 **Remember that a question has a subject and a verb.**
is
Where ᴧ Room 203?

3 **Don't use contractions with short *Yes* answers to *Yes / No* questions.**
I am
"Are you tired?"   "Yes, ~~I'm~~."

4 **Make sure the subject and verb agree.**
Are
~~Is~~ John and Pedro here?

5 **Put the verb after the question word in information questions.**
When is the writing class?
~~When the writing class is?~~

Editing Task

Find and correct the mistakes in these questions and answers about your school.

W
1 ~~w~~here is your school?

2 What is the school's name.

3 How much the tuition is?

4 "your school expensive."   "Yes, it's."

5 What your major?

6 Is you a good student?

7 When summer break is?

8 Is all your classes difficult?

5 Academic Writing

Writing about a Person

Brainstorm > Write > Edit

In this writing cycle (Units 2–4), you are going to answer the prompt below. In this unit (2), you will read an article about a person and then brainstorm ideas for your writing.

> *Write about someone in your family.*

Exercise 5.1 Preparing to Write

Ask and answer questions with a partner.

1 Who are your family members? What are their names?
2 How is your family different from other families? What makes your family unique or special?
3 Why is your family important to you?
4 Are you similar to the people in your family? Are you different?

Exercise 5.2 Focusing on Vocabulary

Read the sentences. Match the words in bold to the definitions.

1 Sultan has an **unusual** job! I have never heard of it.
2 My brother is a student at an English university. He **lives** in London.
3 My father is a teacher. He **works** in a school.
4 My sister is **interested in** languages. She wants to learn Japanese.
5 I like to listen to **music**. I love classic rock and jazz.
6 I **watch** TV at night. I watch basketball games and other sports.
7 On a **normal** day, I go to work. Then I come home and eat dinner with my family.
8 My **family** is big. I have a mother, a father, four sisters, and three brothers.

a _____ (n) a group of people related to each other, such as a mother, a father, and their children
b _____ (adj) usual, ordinary, and expected
c _____ (v) to have a home; to stay in a place
d _____ (adj phr) wanting to learn more about something
e _____ (n) sounds that are made by playing instruments or singing
f _____ (adj) different and not usual; often in a way that is interesting or exciting
g _____ (v) to do a job, especially the job you do to get money
h _____ (v) to look at something for some time

A Very Tall Man

1 Sultan Kösen is from Turkey. He **lives** in Mardin in Turkey. He lives with his **family**. Sultan lives with his mother, his three brothers, and his sister.

2 Sultan is a farmer. His hobby is **watching** TV. He is
5   **interested in music**. His height is **unusual**. He is 8 feet 3 inches (251 cm) tall—that is very tall. Sultan is the tallest man in the world. His mother, brothers, and sister are **normal** height.

3 Sultan **works** on the farm. He has a tractor. His life
10   is not easy. People look at him in the street. Normal clothes and shoes are too small. His clothes and shoes are very big.

4 Sultan speaks Turkish and English. He went to London, Paris, and Madrid in Europe in 2010. He
15   went to New York, Chicago, and Los Angeles in the United States in 2011.

Exercise 5.3 Comprehension Check

Read the text. Work with a partner. Ask and answer the questions.

1 What is Sultan's last name? _____

2 Does Sultan live in Turkey? _____

3 Who is in Sultan's family? _____

4 What are Sultan's hobbies? _____

5 Is Sultan a teacher? _____

6 Is Sultan's life easy? _____

Exercise 5.4 Noticing the Grammar

Work with a partner. Complete the tasks.

1 What *Wh-* question does the first sentence in paragraph 1 answer?
2 What *Wh-* question does the first sentence in paragraph 2 answer?
3 Underline all instances of the verb *be* in paragraph 2. Which are singular? Which is plural?

Using Pronouns to Avoid Repetition

When writers write about a specific person, they include important information about the person's life, such as where the person is from, what his/her family and job are like, and what his/her hobbies are. In addition, writers often use subject pronouns (*he* or *she*) to avoid repeating the person's name.

Sultan is a farmer. **He** is interested in music.

Exercise 5.5 Applying the Skill

Read the sentences. Replace the underlined nouns with *he/she*. Write the sentences again.

1 Sultan Kösen is from Turkey. Sultan lives in Mardin in Turkey. Sultan lives with his mother, his three brothers, and his sister.

_____

_____

2 Sultan works on the farm. Sultan has a tractor.

_____

_____

3 Sultan speaks Turkish and English. Sultan went to London, Paris, and Madrid in 2010.

_____

_____

4 My mother is from Argentina. My mother is an accountant. My mother works in the city.

_____

_____

5 My father is from Russia. My father has a small family. My father has one sister.

_____

_____

My Writing

Brainstorming

Before you write, you need to think of things to write about. This is called **brainstorming**. Brainstorming is the first step in the writing process. You can brainstorm a list of topics to write about or ideas and details about a topic.

Exercise 5.6 Applying the Skill

1 Think of someone in your family. Use the chart to write as much information about the person as possible.

first name	
last name	
date of birth	
city	
country	
family	
job	
hobbies	
languages	

2 Work with a partner and use your chart. Ask and answer questions like the ones in Exercise 5.3 on page 25 about the person in your family.

Count Nouns; *A / An*; *Have* and *Be*

Gadgets

1 # Grammar in the Real World

ACADEMIC
WRITING

Writing about a
person

A Do you have a smartphone? If so, is your smartphone like these phones? Read the article. Which phone is best for you?

B Comprehension Check Answer the questions. Circle *Yes* or *No*. Use the web page to help you.

1 Are the two phones new models?   Yes   No

2 Is the MAX 3i $129?   Yes   No

3 Is the SmartX 2030's camera good?   Yes   No

C Notice Circle the correct words. Use the web page to help you.

1 The MAX 3i is **a / an** old model.

2 Jen is **a / an** busy person.

3 The battery life is 10 **hour / hours**.

4 This is a great **phone / phones** for me.

www.i-buy.net/electronics/smartphones/compare_products_max3i-smartX2030

GREAT PRICES ON
USED SMARTPHONES

 **VS**

MAX 3i

It's **an** old model, but it **has** all the basic features[1].

SmartX 2030

It's **a** new model and **has** lots of great new features.

PRICE

5   **$159.00**   **$289.99**

FEATURES

It's **a** camera, **a** phone, and **a** GPS. It's **an** amazing deal!

It's **a** phone, **a** browser, **a** camera, **a** TV player, and it has **an** assistant to help you!

☑ Talk!
10 ☑ Text.
☑ Play games!
☑ Listen to music!

☑ Send texts, emails, photos and videos anytime, anyplace.
☑ Read news and weather updates.
☑ Shop online.
☑ Play games.
☑ Watch movies and TV or listen to music.

REVIEWS

 ★★★★☆

15 **Jen:** I'm a busy person, and this is a great phone for me at college. It's perfect for students.

 ★★★★☆

Mei: I'm an artist, and I need a good camera. This phone has **an** excellent camera for photos and video.

★★★☆☆

Niki: I like the size, and it's good for texting and making calls, but the
20 camera isn't very good.

★★★☆☆

Pedro143: The battery life is only 10 **hours** (talk time), so that's not great. But it's a good phone.

[1]**feature:** an important characteristic

2 Nouns; *A/An*

Grammar Presentation

Nouns are words for people, places, and things.	*I'm an* artist. *It's an electronics* store. *It is a great* phone. *They are great* phones.

2.1 Singular and Plural Nouns

SINGULAR	PLURAL
It's a watch. *It's a good* product.	*They are* watches. *They are good* products.

2.2 Singular Nouns

A Count nouns have singular and plural forms.	*a book – three* books *one phone – two* phones
B Use *a* before singular count nouns that begin with a consonant sound (*b, c, d, f, g*, etc.).	*a* cell phone *a* web browser *a* screen *a* camera
C Use *an* before singular count nouns that begin with a vowel sound (*a, e, i, o, u*).	*an* address book *an* advertisement *an* email *an* update
Note: Some nouns that begin with the letter *u* have a consonant sound ("you").	*a* unit *a* university

▶▶ Indefinite and Definite Articles: See page A19.

2.3 Plural Nouns

A Add *-s* to most singular nouns to form plural nouns.	*a model – two* models *a device – two* devices *a key –* keys *a student –* students
B Add *-es* to nouns that end in *-ch, -sh, -ss, -z,* and *-x.*	*watch –* watches *class –* classes *dish –* dishes *tax –* taxes

2.3 Plural Nouns *(continued)*

C With nouns that end in consonant + *y*, change the *y* to *i* and add *-es*.	battery – batteries accessory – accessories
D With nouns that end in *-ife*, change the ending to *-ives*.	life – lives knife – knives

2.4 Irregular Plural Nouns

A Some plural nouns have irregular forms. 🌐 These are the most common irregular plural nouns in academic writing.	man – men woman – women child – children person – people foot – feet tooth – teeth
B Some nouns have the same form for singular and plural.	one fish – two fish one sheep – two sheep
C Some nouns are only plural. They do not have a singular form.	clothes jeans scissors headphones pants sunglasses

▸▸ Spelling Rules for Noun Plurals: See page A2.

2.5 Proper Nouns

Proper nouns are the names of specific people, places, and things. They begin with capital letters.	Jenny Mr. Johns Ms. Thorson Canada Dallas Chester College San Francisco Herald

▸▸ Capitalization and Punctuation Rules: See page A1.

🖥 Grammar Application

Exercise 2.1 *A* or *An*

A Write *a* or *an* next to each noun.

1	_*a*_ pencil	5	_____ address book
2	_____ eraser	6	_____ calculator
3	_____ camera	7	_____ wallet
4	_____ laptop	8	_____ notebook

B Over to You Ask and answer questions about things in the classroom. Use *a* or *an*. Make a list of the new words you learn.

A *What's the word for this in English?*

B *It's a desk. / I don't know. Let's ask the teacher.*

A Look at this store advertisement. Write the plural form of the nouns. For nouns that have only one form, leave the space blank.

Shop at THE MART

This Week's Sale Prices

Electronics

battery_____	$15
calculator_____	$129
headphones_____	$5–$65
cell phone_____	$60–$200
computer_____	$800–$4,000
video camera_____	$400–$1,000

School Supply _ies_

dictionary_____	$19–$49.95
scissors_____	$2.95–$10
notebook_____	$2.99–$17.99

Clothes and Accessory_____

dress_____	$49–$239
belt_____	$24–$89
sunglasses_____	$19.99–$289
purse_____	$29.99–$239
jeans_____	$39–$160

B Pair Work Practice asking and answering questions about the items in A with a partner.

A *How much are the belts?*

B *They're $24–$89.*

For nouns that end in the sounds /s/, /ʃ/, /tʃ/, /dʒ/, /ks/, and /z/, say /əz/ in the plural. These nouns have an extra syllable in the plural form.	**/əz/** /s/ cla**ss** – classes /ʃ/ di**sh** – dishes /tʃ/ wat**ch** – watches /dʒ/ messa**ge** – messages /ks/ bo**x** – boxes /z/ qui**z** – quizzes
For most other nouns, say /s/ or /z/ in the plural.	**/s/ or /z/** boo**k** – books pho**ne** – phones accessor**y** – accessories

A Listen. Check (✓) the nouns with an extra syllable in the plural form.

- ✓ **1** purse – purses
- ☐ **2** bag – bags
- ☐ **3** map – maps
- ☐ **4** door – doors
- ☐ **5** size – sizes
- ☐ **6** computer – computers
- ☐ **7** page – pages
- ☐ **8** closet – closets
- ☐ **9** phone – phones

B Write the plural form of these nouns. Do they have an extra syllable? Check (✓) Yes or No.

	Extra Syllable?				Extra Syllable?	
	Yes	**No**			**Yes**	**No**
1 desk _desks_	☐	☑	**8** brush _____		☐	☐
2 tax _____	☐	☐	**9** dictionary _____		☐	☐
3 monitor _____	☐	☐	**10** match _____		☐	☐
4 case _____	☐	☐	**11** chair _____		☐	☐
5 orange _____	☐	☐	**12** quiz _____		☐	☐
6 penny _____	☐	☐	**13** pen _____		☐	☐
7 student _____	☐	☐	**14** garage _____		☐	☐

Exercise 2.4 Proper Nouns

Write answers to the questions. Use proper nouns.

1 What's the capital of the United States? _It's Washington, D.C._ _____

2 What's your last name? _____

3 What's the name of the street where you live? _____

4 What's the name of your hometown? _____

5 What's the name of your favorite movie? _____

3 *Be* with *A / An* + Noun

Grammar Presentation

3.1 Using *Be* with *A / An* + Noun

A You can use *be* with *a / an* + noun to tell:	*It's a watch. It's an activity tracker, too.*
• what something is.	*It's a great phone.*
• what something is like.	*Jon is a friend from college.*
• who someone is.	*He's a nice guy.*
• what someone is like.	

B You can use *be* + *a / an* + noun to say a person's occupation.	*Jenny is a businesswoman.* *Pedro is an architect.*

C Don't use *a / an* with plural nouns.	*They're cell phones.* NOT *They are a cell phones.*

Pronunciation note: *A* and *an* are not usually stressed. *a* = /ə/ and *an* = /ən/
/ə/ CELL phone   /ən/ ARchitect

Grammar Application

Exercise 3.1 *A / An* + Noun

Complete the conversation with *a* or *an*.

A Is that __*a*__ regular watch? Is it _____ activity
       (1)   (2)
tracker, too?

B Both, It's my new toy. It's _____ smart watch.
                                           (3)

A Cool. Oh, look! Is that _____ message?
                                        (4)

B No, it's _____ text from Jeff.
                    (5)

A Jeff? Is he _____ friend?
                       (6)

B Yes, from high school. He's now _____ engineering student at _____ university in
                                               (7)   (8)
Florida. He's in town with his brother, Dan. Dan's _____ artist.
                                                              (9)

A Wow. So, where are they?

B They're at _____ coffee shop near here. Let's go see them.
                      (10)

A That sounds like fun. Let's get _____ taxi.
                                               (11)

Exercise 3.2 *A / An* + Noun: Occupations

A Match the occupations and the pictures. Write the correct letter next to the names. Then
complete the sentences below. Make some occupations plural.

| a chef | b electrician | c̶ engineer | d mechanic | e pharmacist | f receptionist |

1 Mike __*c*__   **2** Carl _____   **3** Julia _____   **4** Jody and Bryan _____

5 Sarah _____   **6** Ana _____

1 Mike __*is an engineer.*_____

2 Carl _____

3 Julia _____

4 Jody and Bryan _____

5 Sarah _____

6 Ana _____

B Over to You Write sentences about people you know.

1 I am *a student. I'm also a part-time salesclerk.*

2 My friend is _____

3 My neighbor is _____

4 My friends are _____ and _____ . They _____

5 My classmate's name is _____ . He / She _____

6 My _____ is _____
     (family member)

4 Have

Grammar Presentation

Have can show possession. It can also mean "to experience."	He **has** a nice apartment. *(possession)* My friends and I **have** a good time together. *(experience)*

4.1 Have

Subject	Have	
I We You They	**have**	a camera.
He She It	**has**	

4.2 Using Have

A Use *have* + noun to show: • possession or ownership. • relationships. • parts of a whole.	*I* **have** *a car.* *She* **has** *a friend from Chile.* *The website* **has** *helpful links.*
B It can also mean "to experience" or "to take part in an activity."	*We* **have** *fun in class.* *They* **have** *lunch at 12:30.*

⬚ Grammar Application

Complete the sentences. Use *have* or *has*.

1 Big Electric is an electronics store. It usually __*has*__ good prices.

2 The store is very large. It _____ four floors.

3 The first floor _____ computers and phones.

4 The second floor _____ video game consoles and video games.

5 The third and fourth floors _____ TVs, sound systems, and entertainment systems.

6 Big Electric also _____ a website.

7 The website sometimes _____ special sale prices.

8 Customers _____ a lot of fun shopping here.

Complete the sentences from a student essay. Use *have*, *has*, *am*, *is*, or *are*.

My Favorite Gadget

Let me tell you about my computer. It __*is*__ an old laptop, but it _____ a good
(1)   (2)

computer. It only weighs two pounds, so it _____ not very heavy. It _____
(3)   (4)

great speakers, and it also _____ a bright, colorful screen. It _____ great for
(5)   (6)

movies and music. It _____ also good for email. I _____ a student, so my
(7)   (8)

laptop _____ very important for me. I use it to do almost all my homework.
(9)

Of course, this laptop also _____ a webcam, so I use it to talk to my friends in
(10)

Mexico. I _____ a lot of friends there, and we _____ always happy to see each
(11)   (12)

other and talk. Sometimes I _____ problems with my laptop. For example, the
(13)

battery _____ not very good, and the hard drive _____ slow. I want a new one,
(14)   (15)

but good laptops _____ expensive.
(16)

5 Avoid Common Mistakes ⚠

1 **Use *a* or *an* to say a person's job.**

       an
Jody is ⌄artist.

2 **Use *a* or *an* to say what kind of a person someone is.**

      a
She's ⌄nice person.

3 **Use *are* after plural nouns. Remember: *people*, *men*, *women*, and *children* are plural.**

        are
The people in my class is nice.

      are
His children is smart.

4 **Use *are* with two nouns joined with *and*.**

         are
My phone and my laptop is on my desk.

5 **Use *has* with a singular subject.**

     has
Tom have a great laptop.

Editing Task

Find and correct nine more mistakes about the Lim family.

                        are
1 The people in my neighborhood is nice.

2 My neighbors is very friendly.

3 Tom and Nancy Lim is my neighbors.

4 Nancy is computer programmer.

5 Tom is cell phone designer.

6 Their children is Joe and Cathy.

7 Joe and Cathy is students at Hatfield College.

8 Joe is student in the computer department.

9 He have a lot of classes this year.

10 Cathy is busy architecture student.

6 Academic Writing

Writing about a Person

Brainstorm 〉 Write 〉 Edit

In Unit 2, you read an article about a person and then brainstormed ideas for the prompt below. In this unit (3), you will write simple sentences about people.

Write about someone in your family.

Writing Simple Sentences

A simple sentence has a subject and a verb. The sentence is about the subject. The subject is a noun, noun phrase, or pronoun. The verb comes after the subject.

        subject   verb
noun: **Gabriela** is from Colombia.

        subject verb   subject verb
pronoun: **He** is from Beijing. **It** is a big city.

Begin the first word in a sentence with a capital letter (A, B, C). Put a period (.) at the end of the sentence.

He watches TV.

Remember: Sentences tell a complete thought. They always have a subject and a verb.

    subject   verb
✔ Rashid plays soccer.

    subject (missing verb)
✘ Rashid soccer.

Exercise 6.1 Applying the Skill

Put the words in order to make sentences.

1 Zhong Shan / My grandfather's name / is / .

_____

2 is / He / 59 / .

_____

3 a doctor / He / is / .

_____

4 is / He / from Hong Kong / .

_____

5 two daughters / He / has / .

_____

6 my mother and father / lives with / He / .

_____

Exercise 6.2 Correcting Sentences

Correct the mistakes in the simple sentences. Compare your answers with a partner's.

1 my name is Gustavo

_____

2 i from Ecuador

_____

3 my father's name Marcus

_____

4 he have two sons

_____

5 my sister's name is Paula

_____

My Writing

Exercise 6.3 Writing Your Sentences

Look at the information in your chart on page 27. Write eight sentences about the person in your family. Use a pronoun so you do not repeat the person's name in every sentence.

1 _____

2 _____

3 _____

4 _____

5 _____

6 _____

7 _____

8 _____

Demonstratives and Possessives

The Workplace

1 Grammar in the Real World

ACADEMIC WRITING

Writing about a person

A Can you name five things that you use in an office? Read the conversation. How many different office things do the speakers mention in the conversation?

B Comprehension Check Match the two parts of the sentences about the conversation.

1 Claudia _____   a are in the cabinets.

2 Keung _____   b are his sister's children.

3 The little girls in the photograph _____   c is a new employee.

4 Office supplies _____   d is in the conference room.

5 The meeting _____   e is on her team.

C Notice Find the sentences in the conversation and circle the correct words.

1 The paper is in **these / this** *drawers* below the printers.

2 **Those / That** *photograph* on the left is great.

3 **That / Those** little *girls* are my sister's children.

4 It's **this / these** *way*, down the hall.

Now look at the nouns in *italics*. What words come before the singular nouns? What words come before the plural nouns?

FIRST DAY AT THE OFFICE

Robert   Hello, Claudia. I'm Robert. Welcome to **our** company!

Claudia   Hello, Robert. It's nice to meet you.

5   **Robert**   **This** is **your** desk. **That's** the closet for **your** coat. Let me show you around.

Claudia   Thanks.

Robert   Office supplies, like paper,
10   folders, and pens, are in **those** cabinets over there. The printers are here, and **this** is the only copy machine. The paper is in **these** drawers below
15   the printers.

Claudia   Thanks. **That's** good to know.

Robert   Now, let me introduce you to Keung. He's on **your** team. Keung, **this** is Claudia. She's
20   **our** new sales manager.

Keung   Nice to meet you, Claudia.

Claudia   Nice to meet you, Keung. **Those** photographs are beautiful. Are you a photographer?

Keung   Well, photography is **my** hobby. 25
Those pictures are from **my** trip to Thailand.

Claudia   **That** photograph on the left is great. What is it?

Keung   It's the Royal Palace in Bangkok, 30
my favorite place.

Claudia   **That's** a great picture, too.

Keung   **Those** little girls are **my sister's** children. She lives in Bangkok.

Robert   Sorry to interrupt, but we have 35
a management meeting in 10 minutes. It's in the conference room. It's **this** way, down the hall. Let's get some coffee before the meeting. 40

Claudia   OK. See you later, Keung.

Keung   Wait. Robert, are **these your** reports?

Robert   Yes, they are. Thanks. I need them for the meeting. 45

2 Demonstratives (*This, That, These, Those*)

Grammar Presentation

The demonstratives are *this, that, these,* and *those*. We use demonstratives to "point to" things and people.	*This* is my desk. *Those* desks are for new employees.

2.1 Demonstratives with Singular and Plural Nouns

SINGULAR				
This/That	Noun	Verb		
This	drawer	is	empty.	
That			for paper.	

PLURAL				
These/Those	Noun	Verb		
These	cabinets	are	for supplies.	
Those			locked.	

2.2 Demonstratives Used Without Nouns

SINGULAR		
This/That	Verb	
This	is	for you.
That		my desk.

PLURAL		
These/Those	Verb	
These	are	from your co-workers.
Those		for us.

2.3 Using Demonstratives with Singular and Plural Nouns

A Use *this* for a person or thing <u>near</u> you (a person or thing that is <u>here</u>).	*This* desk is Amanda's. *This* paper is for the printer.
B Use *that* for a person or thing <u>not near</u> you (a person or thing that is <u>there</u>).	*That* desk is Janet's. *That* printer is a 3D printer.
C Use *these* for people or things <u>near</u> you (people or things that are <u>here</u>).	*These* reports are for the meeting. *These* students are in your English class.

2.3 Using Demonstratives with Singular and Plural Nouns *(continued)*

D Use *those* for people or things <u>not near</u> you (people or things that are <u>there</u>).	*Those folders are the sales reports.* *Those soccer players are great.*
E Use *this, that, these,* and *those* before nouns to identify and describe people and things.	*This photo is my favorite.* *That little girl in the photo is my sister's daughter.* *These charts are helpful.* *Those papers are important.*

2.4 Using Demonstratives with *Be*

A You can use *this, that, these,* and *those* as pronouns to identify things.	*This is the only copy machine.* *= This copy machine is the only copy machine.* *That is the color printer.* *= That printer is the color printer.* *These are the reports for the meeting.* *= These reports are the reports for the meeting.* *Those are my keys.* *= Those keys are my keys.*
B You can only use *this* and *these* as pronouns to introduce people.	**A** *This is Claudia.* **B** *Hi, Claudia! Nice to meet you.* **A** *These are my co-workers, Mena and Liz.* **B** *Hello. Nice to meet you.*
C In informal speaking, use the contraction *that's* instead of *that is*.	*That's a nice picture.*

2.5 Questions with Demonstratives

A To identify people, ask questions with *Who is . . . ?* If it's clear who you are talking about, you can omit the noun.	*Who is that new teacher?* *Who is that?*
B To identify things, ask questions with *What is . . . ?* If it's clear what you are talking about, you can omit the noun.	*What is that noise?* *What is that?*

C To ask about a price, use *How much is/are . . . ?* If it's clear what you are talking about, you can omit the noun.	*How much is* this printer? *How much is* this? *How much are* these printers? *How much are* these?
D After questions with *this* and *that*, answer with *it* for things and *he* or *she* for people.	"How much is *this* copier?" "*It*'s $400." "Who is *that* woman?" "*She*'s my boss."
E After questions with *these* and *those*, answer with *they*.	"Are *these* your reports?" "Yes, *they* are." "Who are *those* people?" "*They*'re my co-workers."

Grammar Application

Exercise 2.1 Demonstratives with Singular and Plural Nouns

Help Margo describe her office. Write *this* or *these* for things that are near her, and *that* or *those* for things that are **not** near her.

1 ____This____ phone is old.

2 _____ closet is for her coat.

3 _____ books are about business.

4 _____ computer is old.

5 _____ pens are very good.

6 _____ window is open.

7 _____ papers are for the meeting.

8 _____ cabinet is for paper clips, folders, and general office things.

9 _____ picture is a photograph of her family.

10 _____ folders are for the sales reports.

Exercise 2.2 More Demonstratives with Singular and Plural Nouns

Pair Work **What's in your pocket? What's in your bag? Tell your partner using** *this* **and** *these*. **Then your partner repeats everything using** *that* **and** *those*.

A *This is a cell phone. These are keys. This is a pen. These are pencils. This is a paper clip.*

B *OK. That's a cell phone. Those are keys. That's a pen. Those are pencils. That's a paper clip.*

Exercise 2.3 Demonstratives Without Nouns

A Which noun isn't necessary? Cross out the noun. Check (✓) the sentences where you cannot cross out the noun.

Jane	How much are these (1) ~~flash drives~~?
Salesclerk	$30.
Jane	Thank you. That's a nice (2) *computer.* ✓
Lisa	Yes, it has a big screen. What's that (3) *thing* on the front?
Salesclerk	It's the webcam. And here's the headphone jack.
Jane	Yeah. Is this (4) *model* a new model?
Salesclerk	No. This (5) *model* is an old model. That's why it's on sale. That's (6) *the new model* over there.
Jane	Oh, I see. Hey, these (7) *headphones* are great headphones.
Lisa	Yeah? Buy them!
Jane	Hmm . . . They're $250. No, thank you!

B Listen to the conversation and check your answers.

Exercise 2.4 Questions and Answers with Demonstratives

Circle the correct words.

1 **A** How much is **these /** (**that**) printer, please? **B** (**It's** / **They're** $220.

2 **A** Excuse me, how much are **these / this** scanners? **B** **It's / They're** $250.

3 **A** How much is **those / this** projector? **B** **It's / They're** $899.

4 **A** Excuse me, how much are **that / those** pens? **B** **It's / They're** $7.99.

5 **A** How much are **these / that** laptops? **B** **It's / They're** on sale. **It's / They're** $1,100.

6 **A** How much is **those / that** digital photo frame? **B** **It's / They're** $80.

Pair Work **Look around your classroom. In each box, write the names of three more things you see.**

	Near Me	**Not Near Me**
Singular	*a desk, . . .*	*a map, . . .*
Plural	*books, . . .*	*windows, . . .*

Ask your partner *Yes/No* questions about the things above. Answer with *it* (singular) or *they* (plural).

A *Is that a map of Iowa?*

B *No, it's not. It's a map of Illinois.*

A *Are these books new?*

B *Yes, they are.*

You can use short responses with *That's* + adjective in conversations.	**A** I have a new job. **B** *That's great! / That's good!*	**A** My printer is broken. **B** *That's too bad.*
Here are common adjectives to use with *that's*.	excellent good great OK terrible too bad	interesting nice wonderful

Write a response with *That's* + adjective. Use the adjectives above.

1 It's a holiday tomorrow. <u>*That's nice.*</u>

2 We're on the same team! _____

3 Business isn't very good this year. _____

4 Patricia's not here today. She's sick. _____

5 I have a new laptop! _____

6 This phone has a dictionary app. _____

3 Possessives and *Whose*

Grammar Presentation

<table>
<tr>
<td>Possessives show that someone possesses (owns or has) something.</td>
<td>

A *Is this Diane's desk?*

B *No, it's my desk. Her desk is in the other office. Her boss's desk is in that office, too.*

</td>
</tr>
</table>

3.1 My, Your, His, Her, Its, Our, Their

Subject	Possessive	
I	my	I'm not ready for the meeting. *My* presentation isn't finished.
you	your	You are very organized. *Your* space is so neat.
he	his	He is a new employee. *His* old job was in Hong Kong.
she	her	She isn't in the office now. *Her* computer is off.
it	its	It is a technology start-up. *Its* CEO is Prima Janesh.
we	our	We have the reports. *Our* boss wants to read them now.
you	your	You are co-workers. *Your* office is on the second floor.
they	their	They are at the office. *Their* boss is on vacation.

▸▸ Subject and Object Pronouns: See page A18.

3.2 Possessive Nouns

A Add 's to singular nouns to show possession.	*The manager's name (one manager)* *The boss's ideas (one boss)*
B Add an apostrophe (') to plural nouns ending in -s to show possession.	*The managers' names (more than one manager)* *The bosses' ideas (more than one boss)*
C For irregular plural nouns, add 's to show possession.	*The men's books (more than one man)* *The children's room (more than one child)*
D *My, your, his, her, our,* and *their* can come before a possessive noun.	*my friend's job* *our parents' names*

▸▸ Capitalization and Punctuation Rules: See page A1.

3.3 Whose?

A We can use *whose* to ask who owns something. We can use it with singular and plural nouns.	*Whose jacket is this?* *I think that's Kana's jacket.*
B We often use *whose* with *this, that, these,* and *those.*	*Whose papers are those?* *Oh! They're my papers. Thank you.*

3.4 Using Possessives

A Use the same possessive form before a singular noun or a plural noun.	**SINGULAR** *my friend* *her report* *the boss's report*	**PLURAL** *my friends* *her reports* *the boss's reports*
B Use a possessive to show that someone owns something.	*her pen* *their folders* *Rachel's car*	
C Use a possessive to show that someone has something.	*your name* *my birthday* *Jared's job*	
D Use a possessive to show relationships between people.	*my sister* *his boss* *Claudia's co-worker*	
E Use a possessive noun to talk about places and countries.	*The city's population* *Japan's prime minister*	

Grammar Application

Exercise 3.1 Possessives

Ben sends an e-mail to Dora and attaches some pictures. He describes them. Complete the e-mail. Use the possessive form of the pronoun in parentheses – *my, his, her, its, our, their* – or *'s*.

Hi Dora,

Here are the photos of __*our*__ (we) end-of-semester party
(1)

for _____ (we) English class. The first photo is Juliana
(2)

and Sue-jin. Is Juliana in _____ (you) math class?
(3)

5 She's sometimes _____ (I) partner in pair work.
(4)

Sue-jin is _____ (she) best friend.
(5)

Then, in the second photo, the woman in the white

shirt is Sally. She's _____ (Juliana) sister. _____
(6) (7)

(They) family is in Chicago, but Sally is here, too. The tall

10 man is Mr. Donovan. He's _____ (we) new teacher.
(8)

_____ (He) first name is Howard, and he's very
(9)

friendly. In this photo we're in the hall near _____
(10)

(Mr. Donovan) office. Send me some pictures of

your class.

15 Ben

A Circle the correct form of the possessive ('s or s') in the sentences.

1 My **co-worker's/co-workers'** name is Krista.

2 **Krista's/Kristas'** last name is Logan.

3 She has two managers. Her **manager's/managers'** names are Tom and Sara.

4 **Sara's/Saras'** family is from Colombia.

5 She has two brothers. Her **brother's/brothers'** names are José and Carlos.

6 **Tom's/Toms'** wife is from New Jersey. Her name is Jessica.

7 Jessica and Tom have a daughter. Their **daughter's/daughters'** name is Danielle.

8 They have two cats. The **cat's/cats'** names are Sam and Max.

B Pair Work Tell a partner about someone you know at work or about a friend at school.
Use the sentences in A as a model.

A Complete the questions about the people in the photos with *Whose* and *Who's*. Then answer the questions.

Name: Ling Yang
Nationality: Chinese
Birthday: October 2
Best friend: Leila
Major: Nursing
Interests: yoga, art

Name: Ki-woon Do
Nationality: South Korean
Birthday: June 5
Best friend: Nora
Major: Business
Interests: soccer, movies

Name: Missolle Beauge
Nationality: Haitian
Birthday: April 7
Best friend: Lona
Major: Computers and
Technology
Interests: music, cooking

1 ____*Whose*____ best friend is Leila?   _Leila is Ling's best friend._

2 _____ birthday is in June?   _____

3 _____ Chinese?   _____

4 _____ major is Business?   _____

5 _____ Haitian?   _____

6 _____ from South Korea?   _____

7 _____ major is Nursing?   _____

8 _____ birthday is in October?   _____

9 _____ interested in soccer?   _____

10 _____ interests are music and cooking?   _____

B Pair Work Ask and answer other questions about the people in A.

A *Whose best friend is Nora?*
B *Nora is Ki-woon's best friend.*

4 Avoid Common Mistakes ⚠

1 **Use *this* and *that* for singular things and people.**
   This
~~These~~ printer is $179.
   That
~~Those~~ man is my manager.

2 **Use *these* and *those* for plural things and people.**
   These
~~This~~ folders are for the meeting.
   Those
~~That~~ women are on my team.

3 ***Its* is possessive. *It's* is a contraction for *it is*.**
                                Its   *It's*
He works for a small company. ~~It's~~ name is Z-Tech. ~~Its~~ on Main Street.

4 **Use *'s* (singular) or *s'* (plural) with possessive nouns.**
              mother's   *co-workers'*
Tomorrow is her ~~mother~~ birthday.   I don't know my ~~co-workers~~ birthdays.

5 **Use the same possessive form before a singular noun or a plural noun.**
                                  her
Justine enjoys spending time with ~~hers~~ co-workers.

Editing Task

Find and correct eight more mistakes in this conversation.

A Hi. I'm sorry to interrupt you, but where's the manager office?
                                                                    's

B Its next to Claudia office.

A Where is those? I don't know Claudia.

B Oh, it's down these hallway right here. Turn left after you pass that two elevators.

A Oh, OK. You mean its near the two assistants office.

B That's right. Do you know them?

A Yes, I do.

B Then please give them a message. Theirs folders are on my desk.

5 Academic Writing

Writing about a Person

Brainstorm > Write > **Edit**

In Unit 3, you wrote sentences for the prompt below. In this unit (4), you will learn how to include extra details in sentences. Then you will revise and edit your writing.

> *Write about someone in your family.*

Adding Details with *and*

When writers revise, they often add new details to make their ideas more interesting to the reader. Writers often add new ideas with **and**. You can use *and* to combine nouns, verbs, and adjectives.

Lucas is interested in music ➔ Lucas is interested in music **and** art. (two nouns)

Lucas works on a farm. ➔ Lucas lives **and** works on a farm. (two verbs)

He is tall. ➔ He is tall **and** thin. (two adjectives)

When writers combine three ideas with *and*, they add commas between the ideas: Lucas lives with his parents, his brother, **and** his grandmother.

Don't use more than one *and* in a sentence.

Exercise 5.1 Understanding the Skill

Make sentences with the words and phrases. Use *and* to add details, and add commas if necessary. Make any other changes to make the sentences correct.

1 My uncle / interested in / art / photography
   My uncle is interested in art and photography.

2 He / live / work / in London
   _____

3 He / smart / creative
   _____

4 He / have / daughter / son
   _____

5 He / live with / his wife / two children / dog
   _____

6 He / happy / successful / caring
   _____

My Writing

Exercise 5.2 Applying the Skill

Review your sentences in My Writing on page 39. Think of some new information about the person. Use *and* to add these new details to at least two of your sentences.

Exercise 5.3 Revising Your Ideas

1 Work with a partner. Use the questions below to give feedback on the ideas in your partner's sentences.

- What information in your partner's sentences is the most interesting to you?
- Is any of the information in your partner's sentences unnecessary or unclear?
- What information would you like your partner to add?

2 Use the feedback from your partner to revise your sentences.

Exercise 5.4 Editing Your Writing

Use the checklist to review and edit your sentences.

Does each sentence have a subject and a verb?	
Does each sentence begin with a capital letter and end with a period?	
Did you use 's (singular) or s' (plural) with possessive nouns?	
Did you use the same possessive form before a singular noun or a plural noun?	
Did you use pronouns to avoid repetition?	
Did you use *and* to add new details?	

Descriptive Adjectives

1 Grammar in the Real World

ACADEMIC
WRITING

Writing about a
place

A Do you use a social networking website? Which one? Read the web article about a social networking site for jobs. Are these websites useful for employers?

B Comprehension Check Answer the questions. Use the article to help you.

1 What is JobsLink?

2 Is Julia a student or an instructor?

3 Is Ricardo an employee or an employer?

4 Who has an interview with Ricardo?

C Notice The nouns in each sentence are underlined. Circle the word that describes each noun. These words are adjectives.

1 Companies can find new workers.

2 He has a small business.

3 Julia is a hardworking student at a large community college.

4 Julia has a new job.

Do the adjectives come before or after the nouns?

USING SOCIAL MEDIA
FOR JOBS

Sometimes, social networking websites[1] are for sending news, messages, and photos to friends. They're like **big** bulletin boards on the Internet. Now social networking websites are for work, too. **Unemployed**[2] people can find jobs there, and companies can find **new**
5 workers. Some sites also have a lot of very **useful** information about jobs and careers.

Here is the story of two people who use JobsLink, a social networking website for business professionals.

Julia is a **hardworking** student at a **large** community college. She's
10 very **busy** with her courses, but she is also **ambitious**.[3] Her career goal is to be an accountant. She has a profile on JobsLink. Her profile has a link[4] to her résumé.

Ricardo is an employer. He has a **small** business. His accounting office needs a **new** accountant. He's interested in Julia's profile on
15 JobsLink. She's **young**, but she's an **excellent** student. Ricardo contacts Julia by e-mail. She has an interview with Ricardo. He thinks that Julia is **friendly** and **smart**. Soon, Julia has a **new** job. Julia and Ricardo are **happy** with JobsLink.

[1]**social networking websites:** places on the Internet for meeting and talking to people

[2]**unemployed:** not having a job that earns money

[3]**ambitious:** wanting success

[4]**link:** a word or image on a website that can take you to another document or website

2 Adjectives

Grammar Presentation

Adjectives describe or give information about nouns – people, places, things, and ideas.	I found a *good* job. (*Good* describes *job*.) This website is *helpful*. (*Helpful* describes *this website*.)

2.1 Adjectives

A Adjectives can come before nouns.

	ADJECTIVE	NOUN
He owns a	*small*	*business*.
She has a	*new*	*job*.

B Adjectives can come after the verb *be*. They describe the subject.

SUBJECT	BE	ADJECTIVE
Julia	*is*	*smart*.
They	*are*	*young*.

C Adjectives have the same form when they describe singular or plural nouns.

	ADJECTIVE	NOUN (SINGULAR)
He needs a	*good*	*accountant*.
	ADJECTIVE	NOUN (PLURAL)
He needs two	*good*	*accountants*.

2.2 Using Adjectives

A When using an adjective before a singular noun:
- use *a* before adjectives that begin with a consonant[1] sound.

They work for a big company.
She has a long résumé.
A new student is in my class.

- use *an* before adjectives that begin with a vowel[2] sound.

He has an interesting blog.
She's an ambitious businessperson.
That's an excellent idea!

B You can use adjectives to describe:
- color
- age
- size
- shape
- opinions
- length of time

a *blue* suit	an *orange* skirt
a *new* website	an *old* résumé
a *tall* building	a *small* phone
a *wide* street	a *round* window
a *great* job	an *excellent* student
a *short* meeting	a *long* vacation

C You can use *very* to make the adjective stronger.

The meeting was very long.

Reminder:
[1]**Consonants:** the letters *b, c, d, f, g, h, j, k, l, m, n, p, q, r, s, t, v, w, x, y, z*
[2]**Vowels:** the letters *a, e, i, o, u*

DATA FROM THE REAL WORLD

These adjectives are used after the verb *be*.
Do *not* use them before a noun.

afraid, alone, asleep, awake
Ahmed is asleep.
NOT *Ahmed is ~~the asleep man~~.*

 # Grammar Application

Exercise 2.1 Adjective + Noun

A Rewrite the sentences with the adjectives in parentheses.

1 James is an engineer. (unemployed) *James is an unemployed engineer.*

2 James is a person. (hardworking) _____

3 This is a website. (useful) _____

4 It has jobs. (interesting) _____

5 This is a company. (large) _____

6 James can send his résumé. (new) _____

B Write sentences about the people and things in parentheses. Use your own ideas and some of the adjectives from the box. Remember to put the adjectives before the nouns.

ambitious	busy	friendly	interesting	popular	unusual
big	difficult	good	kind	smart	useful

1 (company) *Microsoft is a big company.*

2 (person) _____

3 (website) _____

4 (job) _____

5 (employer) _____

6 (student) _____

asleep / awake	good / bad	old / new (things)	*My office isn't loud. It's quiet.*
big / little	happy / sad	old / young (people or animals)	*Please be early. Don't be late.*
big / small	hot / cold	short / long	*This résumé is old, but that one*
early / late	loud / quiet	short / tall	*is new.*

Note: *Big* has two opposites, *little* and *small*. *Short* has two opposites, *tall* and *long*. *Tall* is for height. *Long* is for length, distance, or time.
Old has two opposites, *new* and *young*. *New* is for things, and *young* is for people or animals.

A Complete the sentences with their opposites. Use adjectives from the Vocabulary Focus box.

1 I'm not asleep right now. I'm ___awake___ .

2 This is a _____ resumé.
It's not old.

3 The office is very _____ .
There are only two people here.
It isn't big.

4 The office building is _____ .
It isn't short. It has 50 floors.

5 Today isn't bad. This is a _____ day!
I have a new job!

6 Do you have a _____ ruler?
This one is short.

B Pair Work Work with a partner. Make sentences with adjectives from the Vocabulary Focus box. Your partner makes sentences with the opposite adjectives. Take turns.

A *This isn't a <u>little</u> book.*
B *It's a <u>big</u> book.*

A *I'm <u>tall</u>.*
B *Maria is <u>short</u>.*

C Complete the e-mail. Use the adjectives from the box.

excited	happy	interesting	long	young
friendly	helpful	late	old	

Hi Ramon,

How are you? I'm very ___excited___ about my new job. My work hours are _____ .
(1)   (2)
For example, I usually work from 8:00 a.m. until 6:00 p.m.

But I'm _____ because it's an _____ job. I am a research assistant
(3)   (4)
in a hospital. My office is on the tenth floor. It's an _____ building.
(5)
It's 60 years old. My boss is _____ – he's only 30. He's _____ and
(6)   (7)
_____ when I have questions.
(8)
That's all for now. It's _____ at night and I'm tired. Please write soon.
(9)

Take care,

Jack

Ending in *-an* or *-ian*		Ending in *-ish*	Ending in *-ese*	Ending in *-i*
African	Indian	British	Chinese	Iraqi
American	Indonesian	Danish	Japanese	Israeli
Australian	Italian	English	Lebanese	Kuwaiti
Austrian	Korean	Irish	Portuguese	Omani
Brazilian	Mexican	Polish	Sudanese	Pakistani
Canadian	Nigerian	Scottish	Vietnamese	Qatari
Chilean	Peruvian	Spanish		Saudi
Egyptian	Russian	Swedish		Yemeni
Ethiopian	Syrian	Turkish		
German	Venezuelan			

Exceptions: Dutch (from the Netherlands), Filipino (from the Philippines), French (from France), Greek (from Greece), Swiss (from Switzerland), Thai (from Thailand)

A Complete the sentences. Use nationality adjectives.

1 Paula is from Brazil. She's ___*Brazilian*___ .

2 My co-workers are from Chile. They're _____ .

3 Hakim is from Kuwait. He's _____ .

4 Alex is from Germany. He's _____ .

5 Vinh is from Vietnam. He's _____ .

6 Sarah is from England. She's _____ .

B Over to You Write three sentences about yourself. Then write sentences about three people from other countries. Remember to capitalize the names of countries and languages.

My name is Claudia. I'm from Mexico. I'm Mexican.

3 Questions with *What . . . like?* and *How + Adjective*

Grammar Presentation

Questions with *What . . . like?* and *How +* adjective ask for a description. They are usually answered with an adjective.	**A** "*What* is Arizona *like*?" **B** "It's *beautiful*." **A** "*How deep* is the Grand Canyon?" **B** "It's *very deep*."

3.1 Questions with *What . . . like?*

What + Be	Subject	*Like*	Answers with Adjectives
What is **What's**	New York	**like**?	It's **big**.
What are	the restaurants		They're **expensive**.

3.2 Questions with *How + Adjective*

How	Adjective	*Be*	Subject	Answers with Adjectives
How	**old**	is	the company?	It's 40 years **old**.
	tall	is	Jack?	He's 6 feet (1.80 meters) **tall**.
	long	are	the lines?	They're not **long**. They're very **short**.
	cold	is	the water?	It's not very **cold**. It's **warm**.

Grammar Application

Exercise 3.1 Questions with *What . . . like?*

A Complete the conversation about the city of St. Louis. Use *What . . . like* in the questions. Then choose an answer from the box.

> It's very cold, and it's snowy.   They're good and not too expensive.
> It's an old Midwestern city in Missouri. They're very friendly.

John I have exciting news! I have a new job!

Erica That's great!

John Well, the bad news is this: It's in St. Louis. It's not here in Chicago.

Erica Wow! <u>*What's*</u> St. Louis <u>*like*</u>?

　　　　　　(1)　　　　　　　　(1)

John _____

　　　　　　　　　(2)

Erica _____ the weather _____

　　　　　(3)　　　　　　　　　　　(3)

in the winter?

John _____

　　　　　　　　　(4)

Erica _____ the people _____?

　　　　(5)　　　　　　　　　　(5)

John _____
(6)

Erica _____ the restaurants _____?
(7)   (7)

John _____
(8)

B Listen to the conversation and check your answers.

C Over to You **Write questions with *What . . . like in your city?* Then answer the questions with *It's* or *They're*.**

1 (the weather)　　　　**A** *What's the weather like in your city?*

　　　　　　　　　　　B *It's very hot in the summer.*

2 (the traffic)　　　　　**A** _____

　　　　　　　　　　　B _____

3 (the people)　　　　　**A** _____

　　　　　　　　　　　B _____

4 (the shopping)　　　　**A** _____

　　　　　　　　　　　B _____

5 (the restaurants)　　　**A** _____

　　　　　　　　　　　B _____

6 (the nightlife)　　　　**A** _____

　　　　　　　　　　　B _____

7 (the winters)　　　　　**A** _____

　　　　　　　　　　　B _____

8 (the public transportation)　**A** _____

　　　　　　　　　　　B _____

D Pair Work **Ask and answer questions with a partner.**

A Complete these questions with *How* and an adjective from the box.

bad	cold	crowded	expensive	hot	old

1 _____*How old*_____ is your city?

2 _____ is it in the summer?

3 _____ is it in the winter?

4 _____ is the downtown area with people?

5 _____ are the apartments?

6 _____ is the traffic?

B Write the answers to the questions above about your city. Then ask and answer the questions with a partner.

1 _____

2 _____

3 _____

4 _____

5 _____

6 _____

A *How old is your city?*   **B** *It's really old. It's about 200 years old.*

C Pair Work Write six questions about a city to ask your partner. Write two with *What . . . like?* and three with *How + adjective*. Your partner chooses a city. Then you ask the questions and guess the city.

1 What *are winters like in this city?* _____

2 What _____

3 What _____

4 How _____

5 How _____

6 How _____

7 Let me guess. Is this city _____

4 Avoid Common Mistakes ⚠

1   **An adjective can come before the noun it describes or after the verb *be*.**

     long meeting   *is*
I have a ~~meeting long~~ every Wednesday. This meeting important.

2   **Adjectives do not have plural forms.**

     wonderful
I have three ~~wonderfuls~~ employees.

3   **Use *an* before adjectives that begin with a vowel sound. Use *a* before adjectives that begin with a consonant sound.**

     an   *a*
My sister is ~~a~~ ambitious person. She's ~~an~~ hardworking employee.

4   **Nationality adjectives begin with a capital letter.**

     Danish
Sven is from Denmark. He's ~~danish~~.

Editing Task

Find and correct nine more mistakes in these profiles from a social networking website.

                 Brazilian
My name is Enrique. I'm ~~brazilian~~. My company is called WeMeet. We connect people with similars interests. Users find a interesting topic and sign up to go to a meeting. Some travelers business use WeMeet to find customers, but most people go to make news friends.

My name is Miho. I Japanese. I'm a saleswoman in a japanese robotics company. We make helpfuls robots. We have a ambitious plan to give everyone a robot personal for their home.

5 Academic Writing

Writing about a Place

Brainstorm > Organize > Write > Edit

In this writing cycle (Units 5-7), you are going to answer the prompt below. In this unit (5), you will look at paragraphs about a place and then brainstorm ideas for your writing.

> Write about your country.

Exercise 5.1 Preparing to Write

Work with a partner. Ask and answer the questions.

1 What are some important businesses in your country?
2 How many people live in your country?
3 What is the weather like in your country?
4 What languages do people speak in your country?

Exercise 5.2 Focusing on Vocabulary

Read the sentences. Match the words in bold to the definitions.

1 Jamaica is a tropical **island** in the Caribbean Sea.
2 Kingston is the **capital** of Jamaica. It is the most important city.
3 Many people enjoy the water and sun at the **beach**.
4 **Modern** cities have new buildings, parks, and businesses.
5 Jamaica is **famous** for its beaches. Many people visit them.
6 **Tourists** visit the Jamaica for its good climate.
7 The city is very **international**. People from all over the world live there.
8 Jerk chicken is a **popular** dish in Jamaica. Many people like it.

a _____ (n) people who travel and visit places for fun
b _____ (adj) using new, current ideas or designs
c _____ (n) land with water all around it
d _____ (n) an area of sand or rocks next to a sea, ocean, or lake
e _____ (n) the city where the government is, often the biggest city in a country
f _____ (adj) known and recognized by many people
g _____ (adj) liked by many people
h _____ (adj) relating to or involving two or more countries

The Maldives

The Maldives are tropical **islands** in the Indian Ocean. The islands are near Sri Lanka. The Maldives are **famous** for their good climate, beautiful **beaches**, and warm seas. There are 370,000 people
5 in the Maldives. Most people live on small islands.

The **capital** of the Maldives is Malé. It is a **modern** city with an **international** airport and a big harbor. People in Malé speak English and Dhivehi. English is useful because many **tourists** visit the Maldives.

10 Tourism and fishing are the most important businesses in the Maldives. There are many hotels. Many people work there. Others work as fishermen or in fish factories.

The Maldives are famous for their fish. There
15 is a **popular** fish soup here. It is called *garudiya*. It is delicious.

Exercise 5.3 Comprehension Check

Read the text. Write *T* (true) or *F* (false) next to the statements. Correct the false statements.

_____ 1 The Maldives are famous for their mountains.
_____ 2 English is not very useful in the Maldives.
_____ 3 Many people in the Maldives work in fish factories.

Exercise 5.4 Noticing the Grammar and Structure

Work with a partner. Complete the tasks.

1 Circle the adjectives in the article. Do the adjectives make the article more interesting?
2 Look at the first sentence of each paragraph. What are the topics of the paragraphs?

Paragraph 1: _____

Paragraph 2: _____

Paragraph 3: _____

Paragraph 4: _____

Identifying Main Ideas

Most texts have paragraphs. A paragraph is a group of sentences. Each paragraph has a **topic** and a **main idea**. The topic is what the paragraph is about, for example, the weather. The main idea is the most important idea of the paragraph, for example, *what* about the weather? Main ideas express the writer's opinion or observation about the topic. Writers often use adjectives to give their opinion or observation. Some examples are *important*, *famous*, *interesting*, *exciting*, and *useful*.

Look at paragraph 3 from the text.

> Tourism and fishing are the most important businesses in the Maldives. There are many hotels. Many people work there. Others work as fishermen or in fish factories.

The topic is tourism and fishing. The main idea is that tourism and fishing are the most important businesses in the Maldives. The other sentences in the paragraph are details that support the main idea.

Exercise 5.5 Applying the Skill

Underline the descriptive adjective in each sentence. Then find two details from the reading to support each main idea.

1 The Maldives are a small country.

a _____

b _____

2 The Maldives are famous for their fish.

a _____

b _____

Classifying

Classifying means putting words into groups with the same topic. For example, a writer brainstorms words to describe the Maldives.

tourism   language   fishing   Dhivehi   business   English

Then the writer classifies the words to organize, plan, and discuss the topic.

topic	key words	
business	tourism	fishing
language	English	Dhivehi

Classifying helps you plan your writing.

Exercise 5.6 Applying the Skill

Read the text on page 65 again. Then circle the key words in the chart that the writer used to discuss each topic.

topic	key words
geography	islands climate food Indian Ocean near Sri Lanka
language	English Thai Dhivehi
business	tourism fishing cooking money diving

My Writing

Exercise 5.7 Brainstorming

Brainstorm ideas about your country.

1 Choose three topics from the box. Write them in the first column of the chart.

business   capital   climate   food   geography   language   money   population   sports

topic	key words	adjectives

2 Write key words and adjectives for each topic in the second and third columns.

Exercise 5.8 Writing Sentences

Write two sentences for each topic you chose in Exercise 5.7.

_____
_____
_____
_____
_____
_____

Prepositions

Around the House

1 Grammar in the Real World

ACADEMIC WRITING

Writing about a place

A What's it like to have a houseguest? Maya is away, but her friend Cathy is her houseguest for the weekend. Read Maya's note to Cathy. Do you think Cathy is happy right now?

B Comprehension Check **Match the two parts of the sentences about the note.**

1 Maya is	**a** on the floor.
2 The car is	**b** at her sister's house.
3 The cat food is	**c** in the closet.
4 Clean towels are	**d** out of gas.
5 Cathy is	**e** in the apartment.

C Notice **Complete the sentences. Use the note to help you.**

1 Clean towels and sheets are _____ the closet.

2 The car keys are _____ the refrigerator.

3 The remote control is _____ the counter _____ the coffee maker.

4 See you _____ Sunday evening.

5 My bus arrives _____ 5:30 p.m.

Which sentences tell you when something happens? Which sentences tell you where something is?

Maya's Mess

¹out of gas: without gas

Hi Cathy,

I'm happy you're in the apartment this weekend. My cat Fluffy is glad you're here, too. Please use my bedroom. Clean towels and sheets
5 are in the closet. There's an extra blanket **in** the drawer **under** the bed.

I'm sorry the refrigerator's empty, but the supermarket's **across** the street. The car keys are **on top of** the refrigerator. The car's out of gas,¹
10 but the gas station's close, just two blocks away on Main Street.

The TV's **in** the cabinet **near** the window. The remote control's **on** the counter **next to** the coffee maker. (I think the batteries are dead. ☹)

15 I'm sorry about the cat food **on** the floor. Fluffy's very messy. ☺ The vacuum cleaner's **in** the closet. It's old, but it works. The cleaning supplies are **behind** the plant. The garbage cans are **outside** the front door, **in front of**
20 the garage.

See you **on** Sunday evening. My bus arrives **at** 5:30 p.m, so expect me **between** 6:00 and 7:00.

Love,

25 Maya

P.S. I'm **at** my sister's house. Her phone number is (212) 555-8749.

2 Prepositions of Place: Things at Home and in the Neighborhood

Grammar Presentation

Prepositions can show place. They can tell you where someone or something is.	The remote control is **next to** the coffee maker. My home is **near** the train station.

2.1 Things at Home

in

The vacuum cleaner is **in** the closet.

on / on top of

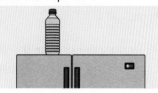

The bottle is **on** the refrigerator.
The bottle is **on top of** the refrigerator.

above

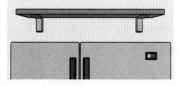

The shelf is **above** the refrigerator.

in front of

The garbage can is **in front of** the garage.

under

The shoes are **under** the bed.

behind

The cleaning supplies are **behind** the plant.

next to / near

The book is **next to** the lamp.
The lamp is **near** the window.

between

The car keys are **between** the watch and the wallet.

2.2 Things in the Neighborhood

in front of

The man is in front of the bakery.

behind

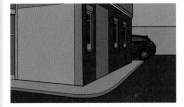

The car is behind the building.

next to / near

The coffee shop is next to the post office.
The coffee shop is near the bakery.

at

The children are at the zoo.

between

The bank is between the restaurant
and the delicatessen.

across from

The woman is across from the bank.

outside

The garbage can is outside the door.

inside

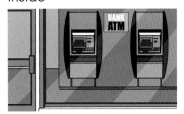

The ATMs are inside the bank.

A Complete the sentences with prepositions of place and the words in the box. Use the picture to help you. Sometimes more than one answer is possible.

coffee maker	counter	door	floor	gym bag	refrigerator	table

Sean I need my cell phone. Where is it?

Jon It's _on the table_ .
(1)

Sean Thanks. Now, where's my gym bag?

Jon It's _____ .
(2)

Sean OK. Oh, and I need my wallet.
Where's that?

Jon It's _____ .
(3)

Sean And my keys. Where are my keys?

Jon They're _____ .
(4)

Sean Now, where's my laptop? I need my laptop.

Jon It's _____ .
(5)

Sean Is the newspaper outside the front door?

Jon No, it's _____ .
(6)

Sean And where are my books for school?

Jon They're _____ .
(7)

Sean Hey. How about a cup of coffee?

Jon Sure. Where's the coffee?

Sean It's _____ .
(8)

B Write questions with *Where* and answers. Use the picture in A to answer the questions.

1 (radio) _Where's his radio? It's on/on top of the refrigerator._

2 (watch) _____

3 (glasses) _____

4 (headphones) _____

5 (notebook) _____

C Pair Work Ask your partner about where things are in his or her home. Write six questions. Then answer your partner's questions. Use the words from the box.

bed	coffee maker	desk	remote control	sofa
clothes	computer	refrigerator	rug	

A *Where's your TV?*   **B** *It's in the living room. It's next to the bookshelf.*

Exercise 2.2 Prepositions of Place: Things in the Neighborhood

A Write sentences about the places in this neighborhood. Use four more of the prepositions from the box.

above	at	between	next to
across from	behind	in front of	outside

1 the gas station / the supermarket *The gas station is behind the supermarket.*
2 the camera store / the shoe store and the coffee shop _____
3 the red car / the gas station _____
4 the shopping carts / the supermarket _____
5 the bookstore / the bank _____

B Listen. Where are these places? Write sentences. Use and reuse the prepositions from the box in A.

1 The parking lot is *in front of the supermarket.*
2 The hair salon is _____
3 The movie theater is _____
4 The park is _____
5 The post office is _____

C Pair Work Ask and answer questions about your school and the area around the school.

A *Where's the post office?*   A *Is the school across from the bank?*
B *It's across from the school.*   B *No, it's next to the library.*

3 Prepositions of Place: Locations and Other Uses

Grammar Presentation

Certain prepositions commonly appear with some locations.	Maya's sister lives *in San Diego*. She lives *on Market Street*. Her home is *at 606 Market Street*.

3.1 In, On, and At with Locations

in + neighborhood . . . + city / town . . . + state . . . + country	I live *in Midtown*. I live *in Miami*. My hometown is *in Ohio*. Montreal is *in Canada*. *What state* is Seattle *in*?
on + street	I live *on Main Street*. The restaurant is *on Grand Avenue*. *What street* is the movie theater *on*?
at + address	I live *at 1298 Seventh Avenue*. We met *at 405 Broadway*.

3.2 Ordinal Numbers with Streets and Floors

1 first	7 seventh	13 thirteenth	19 nineteenth
2 second	8 eighth	14 fourteenth	20 twentieth
3 third	9 ninth	15 fifteenth	21 twenty-first
4 fourth	10 tenth	16 sixteenth	30 thirtieth
5 fifth	11 eleventh	17 seventeenth	31 thirty-first
6 sixth	12 twelfth	18 eighteenth	32 thirty-second

Use ordinal numbers with some streets.	I live on *Third Avenue*. My apartment is on *Ninth Street*.
Use *on* + *the* + ordinal number + *floor*.	The doctor's office is *on the second floor*. I live *on the fifteenth floor*.

3.3 Common Expressions with Prepositions

at home (or home)	Maya is not *at home* this weekend.
	NOT Maya is not ~~at the home~~ this weekend.
at work	She is not *at work* today.
	NOT Maya is not ~~at the work~~ today.
at school / college in school / college	It's 10:30. Cathy's *at school* right now. (= in the building) I'm a student. I'm still *in school*. (= still a student)
in class / in a meeting	Tom is *in class*. (= in the classroom)
on campus	The bookstore is *on campus*.
across the street	The student center is *across the street*.

Grammar Application

Exercise 3.1 *In, On,* and *At* with Locations

A Pair Work **Complete the questions with the correct prepositions. Then write the full answers to the questions. Use your own ideas. Check your answers with a partner.**

1 Are we __*in*__ Canada right now? _____

2 What town or city are we _____ ? _____

3 Are we still _____ Broad Street? _____

4 Are you _____ 25 Madison Avenue? _____

5 Are the restrooms _____ the first floor? _____

6 What street is this school _____ ? _____

B Complete the paragraphs about a student. Use *in, on,* or *at.*

My name is Blanca González, and I am from Mexico. My hometown is __*in*__ Mexico. Now I live
(1)
_____ the United States. I live _____ Waltham,
(2)   (3)
Massachusetts. It's near Boston. My apartment is
_____ 399 Moody Street. My parents also live in
(4)
Waltham, _____ 147 Hope Avenue. They are only
(5)
two minutes away from my apartment.

I have three roommates. Our apartment is _____ the third floor. There
(6)
is a large supermarket _____ my street. There are also several gas stations
(7)
_____ my neighborhood. It's noisy _____ the street, but it's OK _____ our
(8)   (9)   (10)
apartment. During the day I study accounting. In the evenings I work at a restaurant
_____ Watertown. That's a town next to Waltham.
(11)

A Over to You **Complete the information about your home and school. Use the information in parentheses.**

1 My hometown is ____*in*____ ____*Illinois*____ .
   (preposition)   (state or country)

2 My hometown is between _____ and _____ .
   (one city/town)   (another city/town)

3 Now I live _____ _____ .
   (preposition)   (neighborhood)

4 My home is _____ _____ .
   (preposition)   (street name)

5 I live _____ _____ .
   (preposition)   (address – You can give an imaginary address.)

6 My home is near _____ .
   (a place or building)

7 My classroom is _____ _____ _____ floor.
   (preposition) (+ *the*)   (ordinal number)

8 My school is across the street from _____ .
   (a place)

B Pair Work **Share your information with a partner.**

Complete the cell phone conversations. Use *in*, *on*, or *at*. Sometimes more than one answer is possible.

1 **Ashley**   Hi, this is Ashley.

    Sarah   Hi. This is Sarah. Where are you?

    Ashley   I'm __*at*__ work. How about you? Are you _____ home?

    Sarah   No, I'm _____ the movie theater _____ Fourth Street, and I'm cold.

    Ashley   Oh, sorry. I'm late. I'm on my way.

2 **Rodrigo** Hi, it's me.

    Bob   Hi. Where are you? Are you _____ class?

    Rodrigo No. Class starts in two minutes. I'm _____ campus, but I think my backpack's _____ my closet. Can you bring it?

    Bob   Sure. No problem. I'm still _____ the apartment.

3 **Alan** Hey. Where are you? Are you _____ class?

  Inga No. I'm _____ campus. Class starts in five minutes.

  Alan OK. I'm _____ home, but I'll be _____ work tonight.

  Inga OK, thanks for the reminder. I won't wait for you for dinner.

4 **Joseph** Mike? It's Joseph. Are you _____ school today?

  Mike Hi, Joseph. Yes. I'm _____ the library.

  Joseph Well, I'm _____ the coffee shop _____ Sullivan Street. Are you free?

  Mike Sure. See you in five minutes.

4 Prepositions of Time

Grammar Presentation

Prepositions can tell you about when something happens.	Maya returns *on Sunday.* Her bus arrives *at 5:30 p.m.* Cathy expects her *between 6:00 and 7:00.*

4.1 In, On, At

Use *in* + parts of the day	*Cathy always goes for a walk in the afternoon.* *On Mondays, I work in the morning.*	
Use *in* + month	*My birthday is in December.* *Vietnam is beautiful in April.*	
Use *in* + season	*Waltham is very cold in the winter.* *Please visit me in the spring.*	
🌐 People also say, for example, "in winter" and "in spring," but "in the winter" and "in the spring" are more common.		
Use *on* + date In dates, write the number, but say the ordinal number.	*I'll see you on July 1.* *My class ends on May 20.*	(on July first) (on May twentieth)
🌐 People also say, for example, "the twentieth of May," but "May twentieth" is more frequent.		
Use *on* + day	*See you on Monday.* *Our class begins on Friday.*	
Use *at* + specific time	*The bank opens at 7:00.* *I usually wake up at 5:30.*	(at seven / at seven o'clock) (at five-thirty / at half past five)

4.2 Questions with Days, Dates, and Times

You can ask questions about days, dates, or times with:

When is / are . . .
What day is . . .
What time is . . .

You can give shorter or longer answers to questions about days, dates, and times.

"*When is* Independence Day?"
"It's on July 4. / On July 4. / July 4."

"*What time is* your class?"
"It's at 8:00. / At 8:00. / 8:00."

 Grammar Application

A Circle the correct preposition.

1 In my state, it's very cold **at / in** the winter and very hot **at / in** the summer.

2 The warm weather usually starts **on / in** April.

3 Unfortunately, it rains a lot **in / on** the spring.

4 The first day of summer is **in / on** June.

5 In the summer, the sun goes down late **at / in** the evening.

6 It's still sunny when I finish my class **on / at** 7:00.

7 I usually stay up late **on / in** Fridays and look at the stars.

8 I like to wake up **on / at** 6:30 on Saturdays because the weather is still cool **in / at** the morning.

 DATA FROM THE REAL WORLD

People often give approximate times with *around* or *about*.

You can use *between* + two times.

See you around 6:30. (= 6:20–6:40)
Call me about 6:15. (= 6:10–6:20)

I'll see you between 6:00 and 7:00.

B Complete the conversation. Use *in*, *on*, *at*, *around*, or *between*. Sometimes more than one answer is possible.

Alex Let's get together next week. Let's have lunch ___*on*___ Monday. I'm free _____
(1)   (2)

12:30 and 2:30.

Sam Monday? That's my brother's birthday. We always have lunch

together _____ my brother's birthday.
(3)

Alex How about _____ Tuesday?
(4)

Sam Well, I have class _____ the afternoon on Tuesday. It's _____ 1:00.
(5)   (6)

It usually finishes _____ 2:15. Let's meet _____ Wednesday.
(7)   (8)

Alex Great. Let's meet _____ Wednesday then, _____ 1:00.
(9)   (10)

C Over to You Write six sentences about dates that are special for you. Then share your sentences with a partner.

	Date	Why is this date special?
	July 16	My mother's birthday is on July 16.
1		
2		
3		
4		
5		
6		

A *So July 16 is a special date. It's my mother's birthday.*

B *Really? My mother's birthday is in April. It's on April 17.*

A Unscramble the words to make questions about the Expo.

VALE COMMUNITY COLLEGE

MUSIC INDUSTRY EXPO

Thursday, April 22, 7 p.m.–10 p.m.

CONCERT

Friday, April 23, 9 a.m.–5 p.m.

FRIDAY

9:00 Welcome
9:30 "The Business of Music"
10:30 "Becoming a Songwriter"
11:15–11:30 Break
11:30 Talk by Sound Engineer
12:30–1:30 Lunch
1:30 "Writing Music for the Movies"
2:30–4:30 Career Fair
4:30 New Music Software

1 the/Expo/is/When

When is the Expo?

2 day/What/is/the concert

_____

3 the students/do/a break/When/have

_____

4 the Career Fair/What/is/day

_____

5 is/lunch/When

_____

6 the welcome/is/time/What

_____

B Pair Work Ask and answer the questions in A with a partner.

A *When is the Expo?*
B *It's on Thursday, April 22.*

5 Avoid Common Mistakes ⚠

1	**Use *in* + month, but use *on* + date or day.**

       on   *in*   *on*
My birthday is ~~in~~ May 10. My sister's birthday is ~~on~~ May, too, but it's not ~~in~~ the same day.

2	**Use *at* + time.**

              at
My bus arrives ⌄9:00.

3	**Use *on* + street name. Use *at* + address.**

             on   *at*
My house is ~~in~~ Gorge Avenue. It's ~~on~~ 1276 Gorge Avenue.

4	**Use *on* + *the* + ordinal number + *floor*.**

            on the
My office is ~~in~~ third floor.

Editing Task

Find and correct nine more mistakes in this e-mail about a birthday celebration.

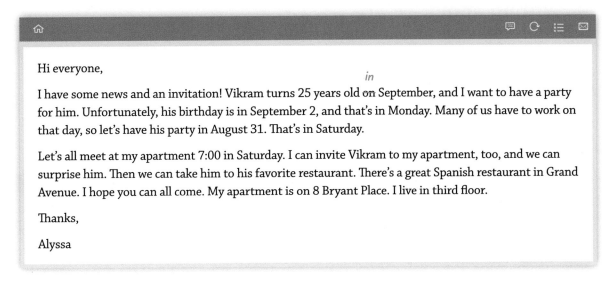

Hi everyone,

I have some news and an invitation! Vikram turns 25 years old ~~on~~ *in* September, and I want to have a party for him. Unfortunately, his birthday is in September 2, and that's in Monday. Many of us have to work on that day, so let's have his party in August 31. That's in Saturday.

Let's all meet at my apartment 7:00 in Saturday. I can invite Vikram to my apartment, too, and we can surprise him. Then we can take him to his favorite restaurant. There's a great Spanish restaurant in Grand Avenue. I hope you can all come. My apartment is on 8 Bryant Place. I live in third floor.

Thanks,

Alyssa

6 Academic Writing

Writing about a Place

Brainstorm > Organize > Write > Edit

In Unit 5, you brainstormed ideas for the prompt below. In this unit (6), you will write topic sentences and complete an outline.

> Write about your country.

Paragraph Structure and Topic Sentences

A **paragraph** is a group of sentences about one main idea. Good paragraphs have three parts: a **topic sentence**, **supporting sentences** with details, and a **concluding sentence**. The topic sentence usually comes first. The details, also called the supporting sentences, come next. The paragraph ends with a concluding sentence.

topic sentence	Life on my island is simple.		
supporting sentences / details	It is a small island south of Malé.	There are some stores and one mosque in my town.	We speak Dhivehi, but we also learn English in high school.
concluding sentence	It is a nice place to live.		

The topic sentence tells the reader the topic and the main idea of the paragraph. In the chart, the topic is life on the writer's island. The main idea is that life is simple there. The next sentences add details to the topic and main idea.

Exercise 6.1 Applying the Skill

Complete the tasks. Then compare your answers with a partner's.

1 Read the paragraph. Underline the topic sentence.

   Tourism and fishing are the most important businesses in the Maldives. There are many hotels. Many people work there. Others work as fishermen or in fish factories.

2 Read the paragraph. Choose the best topic sentence.

   _____ There are many restaurants, and there is a public market. You can buy fresh fish, vegetables, and many other delicious foods there. Everyone loves eating in Barcelona.

   a Eating is an important part of visiting Barcelona.

   b You can do many things in Barcelona.

   c Barcelona is a city in the north of Spain.

Using Prepositional Phrases to Write about Places

When writers describe places, they often use prepositional phrases to give specific details about places, locations, and directions.

Life **on my island** is very simple.

Toronto is the biggest city **in Canada**.

Barcelona is a city **in the north of Spain**.

Exercise 6.2 Applying the Skill

Underline the prepositional phrases of location in the paragraph.

The Maldives are tropical islands in the Indian Ocean. The islands are near Sri Lanka. The Maldives are famous for their good climate, beautiful beaches, and warm seas. There are 370,000 people in the Maldives. Most people live on small islands.

My Writing

Exercise 6.3 Outlining

Review your brainstorming chart on page 67. Use the outline below to organize your notes into three paragraphs about your country. For each paragraph, write a topic sentence and 2-3 supporting sentences/details.

Paragraph 1

Topic Sentence: _____

Supporting Sentences/Details: _____

_____

_____

Paragraph 2

Topic Sentence: _____

Supporting Sentences/Details: _____

_____

_____

Paragraph 3

Topic Sentence: _____

Supporting Sentences/Details: _____

_____

_____

There Is and There Are

Local Attractions

1 Grammar in the Real World

A Do you know a lot about the old areas of your town? Read the blog about a historic street in Los Angeles. What are some fun things to do there?

B Comprehension Check Match the two parts of the sentences about Olvera Street.

1 Olvera Street was	**a** little shops in the area.
2 It's a tourist attraction	**b** interesting things to do.
3 There are a lot of	**c** at noon.
4 There are some	**d** in downtown Los Angeles.
5 The last tour is	**e** a small village in 1781.

C Notice Find these words in the text. Do they come after *there is* or *there are*? Write the words in the correct columns.

a lot of interesting things to do	27 historic buildings
traditional music	a statue of King Carlos III
restaurants	

There is . . .	There are . . .

Now circle the correct words in these two sentences about *there is* and *there are*.

The writer uses ***There is / There are*** with singular nouns. She uses ***There is / There are*** with plural nouns.

Historic Olvera Street

By Marta Ruiz

What is Olvera Street? It's the birthplace of Los Angeles! In 1781, this marketplace was a small village of 44 Mexican settlers.[1] Now it's a popular tourist attraction.[2] It is only one block, but **there are** a lot of interesting things to do.

5 **There are** 27 historic buildings on Olvera Street. **There is** a house that is about 200 years old. **There is** a statue of King Carlos III of Spain and a statue of Felipe de Neve, the first governor[3] of California, in a beautiful plaza.

There are some little shops in the area that sell Mexican clothes, toys, and
10 jewelry. **There are** restaurants with delicious Mexican foods such as *churros* and *enchiladas*. **There is** traditional music and folk dancing on the weekends.

Olvera Street is in downtown Los Angeles, across the street from Union Station. **There are** free tours on most days. Just go to the visitor's center at the Sepulveda House.

15 Come to Olvera Street! Learn about history and experience Mexican culture!

Comments [4]

WorldTraveler78: Are there any public parking lots in the area?

Marta_Ruiz: Yes, **there's** one on Alameda Street,
20 and **there's** one on North Main Street.

LAgirl: Are there any tours in the evening?

Marta_Ruiz: No, **there aren't**. The last tour is at noon.

[1]**settler:** a person who moves to a new country or area
[2]**tourist attraction:** something that makes people want to go to a place
[3]**governor:** a person in charge of a large organization, like a state

2 There Is / There Are

Grammar Presentation

There is and There are tell you that something or someone exists or that something is a fact.	*There's a statue of King Carlos III in this plaza.* *There are free tours on most days.*

2.1 Affirmative Statements

There	Be	Subject	Place/Time	Contraction
There	**is**	a parking lot a free tour	on Alameda Street. at 10:00.	There is → There's
	are	some little shops free tours	in the area. on most days.	

2.2 Negative Statements

There	Be + Not/No	Subject	Place/Time
There	**isn't**	a bank	in Union Station.
	is no	bank	
	isn't	a show	at 8:00.
	is no	show	
	's no	bank	in Union Station.
		show	at 8:00.
	aren't	any cars	on Olvera Street.
	are no	cars	
	aren't	any tours	in the evening.
		tours	

2.3 Using There Is / There Are

A Use *There is / There are* to say that something or someone exists or to introduce a fact or a situation.	*There are a lot of interesting things to do in this area.* *There's an article by Marta Ruiz on this website.* *There are two questions from readers.*
B Use *There is / There are* to tell the location of something or someone.	*There's a parking lot on the corner.* *There are some Mexican restaurants on the next block.* *There's a tour guide at the door.*

2.3 Using *There Is/There Are* (continued)

C	Use *There is/There are* to tell when an event happens.	*There's an art show at 8:00.* *There are concerts on the weekend.*
D	Use the full forms in academic writing, but in speaking, use contractions.	*There's music in the plaza.* *There's no free parking on this street.*
	In informal speech, people often say *There're* instead of *There are*, but don't write it.	*There are a lot of museums in Los Angeles.* NOT *~~There're~~ a lot of museums in Los Angeles.*
E	Use *There is* when there are two or more nouns and the first noun is singular.	SINGULAR NOUN　　　　PLURAL NOUN *There's a jewelry store and two restaurants on this street.*
	Use *There are* when there are two or more nouns and the first noun is plural.	PLURAL NOUN　　　　SINGULAR NOUN *There are two restaurants and a jewelry store on this street.*
F	You can use *some* with a plural noun after *There are.*	*There are some shops around the corner.*
G	For negative statements, you can use *There isn't* and *There aren't.* The full forms *is not* and *are not* are not often used. OR You can use *There is/There are + no.*	*There isn't a bad restaurant on this street.* *There aren't any parking spaces here.* *There's no fee at this parking lot.* *There are no hotels around here.*
	You can use *any* in negative statements with *There aren't.*	*There aren't any traffic lights on Olvera Street.*
H	You can use *There is* and *There are* to introduce new people, places, and things.	INTRODUCTION　　　　MORE INFORMATION *There is an old house on the street. It's now a museum.*
	You can use *It is/It's* and *They are/They're* to give more information.	*There are a lot of shops on Olvera. They are all very nice.*

Grammar Application

A Complete the sentences from an e-mail. Use *There's* or *There are*.

Hi Naoko,

I'm so happy about your visit to Santa Monica. From Los Angeles airport (LAX), _____*there are*_____ several buses
                                                                              (1)
to Santa Monica. Please call me from the bus. I can meet you at the Santa Monica bus station. _____
                                                                                                (2)
a lot of things to see and do here. First, _____ the famous beach. It has a historic pier[1] and some nice
                                            (3)
restaurants. On the beach, _____ volleyball, swimming, and biking. In fact, _____
                            (4)   (5)
even a volleyball competition on Saturday. I know you like surfing, so_____ a surfing school you can
                                                                       (6)
check out. _____ also the Santa Monica Pier Aquarium. My other favorite place is the Third Street
            (7)
Promenade. _____ some great concerts there on the
            (8)
weekend. _____ great stores on the Promenade, too.
          (9)
See you soon!

Kim

[1]pier: a structure over the water where boats can dock

B Over to You What is your favorite city? Fill in the chart with some of the interesting
places in your favorite city.

There is . . .	There are . . .

C Pair Work Tell your partner what is in your favorite city. Use your information from B.
Take turns.

  A *There's an art museum.*
  B *There are several big parks.*

Exercise 2.2 Affirmative and Negative Statements

A Look at the hotel information. Complete the sentences. Use *There is / There are* and *There isn't / There aren't*.

✳ COMFORT HOTEL ✳

- $54 parking (for 24 hours)
- $14.99 wireless Internet service (per day)
- Free breakfast
- Free coffee in the lobby
- Outdoor pool
- Fitness room
- Business services
- Conference center
- Meeting rooms (4)
- Ice machines in the hallways
- Park views
- Restaurant

1 *There isn't* free parking.
2 *There are* business services.
3 _____ an indoor pool.
4 _____ six meeting rooms.
5 _____ any free wireless Internet service.
6 _____ any ocean views.
7 _____ a fitness room.
8 _____ any refrigerators in the rooms.
9 _____ a restaurant.
10 _____ a conference center.

B Over to You What doesn't exist in your town or city? Look at the places in the box. Add your own ideas. Write six sentences about your town or city. Use *There is no* and *There aren't any*.

aquarium	cheap restaurants	historic houses	park	statues
beach	free parking	library	public pool	tourist attractions
bus station	gas stations	museums	river	train station

1 *There aren't any gas stations.*
2 _____
3 _____
4 _____
5 _____
6 _____
7 _____

A Read Mi-Sun's description of her town on her blog. Complete the sentences. Use *There's,* *There are, It's,* or *They're.*

Hi, my name is Mi-Sun. My hometown is Concord, MA. It's a small historic town near Boston.

There are some historic buildings in Concord. _They're_ very old.
(1)   (2)

_____ also a lot of small shops. _____ usually
(3)   (4)

expensive.

_____ an old hotel. _____ called the Colonial Inn.
(5)   (6)

_____ a popular place for lunch and dinner. _____ a
(7)   (8)

lot of special events at the hotel, like weddings and meetings. _____
(9)

often live music at night. I like to go and listen to jazz.

_____ a national park by the Concord River. _____
(10)   (11)

beautiful and peaceful. _____ always a lot of tourists at the park.
(12)

It has a famous bridge – Old North Bridge. Also, _____ a very famous
(13)

statue of a minuteman next to the bridge. The soldier was called a "minuteman"

because he could get ready in a minute. A historic battle happened there in 1775.

I often walk there with friends.

B Listen to Mi-Sun and check your answers.

C Over to You Write four pairs of sentences about your town or city. Use *There's / There* *are* in the first sentence. Use *It's* or *They are* in the second sentence to add more information.

There's a big park in my city. It's on State Street.

1 _____

2 _____

3 _____

4 _____

3 Yes/No Questions with *There Is/There Are*

Grammar Presentation

Yes/No Questions with *There is/There are* can ask about people, things, and events.	*Is there a tour guide in this museum?* *Are there any concerts on Friday?*

3.1 *Yes/No* Questions and Short Answers

Be	There	Subject	Place/Time	Contraction
Is	**there**	a visitor's center	on Olvera Street?	Yes, **there is.**
		a performance	at 6:00?	No, **there isn't.**
Are		any parking lots	in the area?	Yes, **there are**.
		any tours	in the evening?	No, **there aren't**.

3.2 Using *Yes/No* Questions and Short Answers with *There Is/There Are*

A You can use *any* with a plural noun in *Yes/No* questions with *Are there*.	*"Are there any hotels on Alameda Street?"* *"Are there any concerts on weekdays?"*
B In affirmative short answers, don't use the contractions *there's* or *there're*.	*"Yes, there is."* NOT *"Yes, there's."* *"Yes, there are."* NOT *"Yes, there're."*
C You can use *It is/They are* to say more after a short answer.	*"Is there a visitor's center on Olvera Street?"* *"Yes, there is. It is at the Sepulveda House."* *"Are there any parking lots in the area?"* *"Yes, there are. They are on Alameda Street."*

3.3 Longer Answers with *There Is/There Are*

A In longer answers with *There is*, you can use *one* instead of repeating *a* + singular noun.	*Is there a visitor's center on Olvera Street?* *Yes, there's one in the Sepulveda House.* *No, there isn't one on Olvera Street.*
B In longer answers with *There are*, you can use *some/any* instead of repeating *some/any* + plural noun.	*Are there any public parking lots in the area?* *Yes, there are some on Alameda Street.* *No, there aren't any in the area.*

Grammar Application

A Read the TV schedule and complete the questions and answers. Use *Are there any* and *Is there a* for the questions. Then write short answers.

6:30 p.m.	News: *Weather report*	**11:15 p.m.**	Movie: *Where Is Jimmy Jones?*
7:00 p.m.	Talk show: *The Guy Norris Show*	**1:00 a.m.**	Music: *The Dixonville Festival*
8:00 p.m.	Documentary: *Antarctica*	**2:00 a.m.**	Music: *Jazz with Kenny Delmot*
9:00 p.m.	Movie: *The Long Road*	**3:00 a.m.**	Comedy: *The Watson Family*

1 __*Are there any*__ movies on TV tonight?   Yes, there _____ two movies. There's one at 9:00 and one at 11:15.

2 __*Is there a*__ talk show?   Yes, _____ one at 7:00.

3 _____ music shows?   Yes, there _____ . There's one at _____ and one at _____ .

4 _____ sports shows?   _____ .

5 _____ documentary?   _____ one at 8:00.

6 _____ kids' show?   _____ .

7 _____ comedy show?   _____ .

8 _____ news program?   _____ .

B Write questions about events in your city or town. Use *Is there a/an* and *Are there any*.

1 (art festival) _____

2 (jazz concerts) _____

3 (baseball game) _____

4 (dance performance) _____

5 (new paintings at the museum) _____

6 (good movies) _____

C Pair Work Ask and answer the questions with a partner. Write the answers to the questions with your partner.

   A *Are there any good movies this weekend?*
   B *Yes, there are two good movies.*

1 _____
2 _____
3 _____
4 _____
5 _____
6 _____

D Answer each question with *yes* in three different ways. Give information about your own area, if possible.

1 Is there a mall in this town?

   Yes, there's one on Westwood Avenue. Yes, there's a mall on Westwood Avenue.
   Yes, it's on Westwood Avenue.

2 Is there a good coffee shop nearby?

_____

_____

3 Is there an art museum?

_____

_____

4 Is there a nice park?

_____

_____

5 Is there a sports stadium?

_____

_____

6 Is there a big movie theater?

_____

_____

4 Avoid Common Mistakes ⚠

1 Use *There is* with singular nouns. Use *There are* with plural nouns.

        is   *are*
There ~~are~~ a music festival this week.   There ~~is~~ musicians from different countries at the festival.

2 *There is* and *There are* introduce <u>new</u> people, places, and things. *It is* and *They are* give more information.

                                          It
There is a small building on Thomas Street. ~~There~~ is the town museum.
There
~~They~~ are three large cities in Texas. They are Houston, San Antonio, and Dallas.

3 Use the full forms in academic writing. Do not use the contractions.

There is
~~There's~~ a wonderful museum in downtown Philadelphia.
There is
~~There's~~ no bank in the train station.

4 In informal speaking, people often say *There are* very quickly, so it sounds like *They're.* Don't confuse them in writing.

There are
~~They're~~ some great shows this weekend.

Editing Task

Find and correct seven more mistakes in this article about New York City's famous park.

New York City's Central Park

New York City is an expensive place to visit, but there ~~are~~ *is* one place that is always free: Central Park. There is a very big park. In fact, it is about 2.5 miles (4 km) long and 0.5 miles (0.8 km) wide. There is over 843 acres[1] in the park. There is fields, ponds, and lakes. Visitors enjoy different kinds of sports and events here. There are

5 walkers, joggers, skaters, bicyclists, and bird-watchers. There are a zoo and two ice-skating rinks. There's also an outdoor theater. The theater has "Shakespeare in the Park" summer festivals. There is a swimming pool in the summer, too. Throughout the year, they're horse-and-carriage rides. Every year, there is over 25 million visitors. They are happy to visit a fun and free New York City tourist attraction.

[1]**843 acres:** 1.32 square miles or 3.41 square kilometers

5 Academic Writing

Writing about a Place

Brainstorm > Organize > Write > Edit

In Unit 6, you learned about topic sentences and then outlined three paragraphs for the prompt below. In this unit (7), you will write, revise, and edit your paragraphs.

Write about your country.

Using *There Is* and *There Are* to Introduce Details

Writers can use *there is* and *there are* with nouns to introduce specific details about a place. Look at the example below. Notice how the writer uses *there is* and *there are* to give more details about the main idea of the paragraph: eating in Barcelona.

Eating is an important part of visiting Barcelona. **There are** many restaurants, and **there is** a public market in the center of the city. You can buy fresh fish, vegetables, and many other delicious foods there. Everyone loves eating in Barcelona.

Remember: We use *there is* with singular nouns and *there are* with plural nouns.

My Writing

Exercise 5.1 Applying the Skill

Look back at your My Writing on pages 67 and 83. Review your outline. Find at least three places where you can use *there is* or *there are* to add some new information for your paragraphs.

Exercise 5.2 Writing Your Paragraphs

Write three paragraphs about your country. For each paragraph, write a topic sentence, supporting sentences, and a concluding sentence. Use *there is* and *there are* to introduce some of the details.

(1) _____

_____

_____

_____

(2) _____

_____

_____

_____

(3) _____

_____

_____

_____

Exercise 5.3 Revising Your Ideas

1 Work with a partner. Use the questions below to give feedback on the ideas in your partner's paragraphs.

- Which of your partner's ideas are interesting and useful to you?
- Which of your partner's ideas need to be explained more clearly?
- What could your partner add or remove to make the ideas easier to understand?

2 Make any necessary changes to your paragraphs.

Exercise 5.4 Editing Your Writing

Use the checklist to review and edit your paragraphs.

Did you write three paragraphs about your country?	
Did you write a topic sentence with a topic and main idea for each paragraph?	
Did you write 2-3 supporting sentences for each topic sentence?	
Did you write a concluding sentence for each paragraph?	
Did you use descriptive adjectives to make your writing accurate and interesting?	
Did you use prepositional phrases of location correctly?	
Did you use *there is* and *there are* to introduce details?	

Simple Present

Lifestyles

1 Grammar in the Real World

ACADEMIC
WRITING

Writing about
daily life

A Is there someone very old in your family? Read the magazine article about places where people live a long time. Why do some people have a long life?

B Comprehension Check **Answer the questions.**

1 Why do people in some areas live so long?

2 Do these people feel stressed?

3 Do they eat much meat?

C Notice **Find the sentences in the article. Complete the sentences with the correct words.**

1 People in these areas _____ around a lot.

2 They _____ exercise in a gym.

3 They _____ a lot during the day.

4 _____ , they _____ time to rest and relax.

Find the places you use *don't*. **What words show time?**

A Long, Healthy Life

On the Japanese island of Okinawa, many people **live** to be over 100 years old. Researchers[1] **find** this in several places around the world, including Sardinia, Italy; Icaria, Greece; the Nicoya Peninsula of Costa Rica; and Loma Linda, California. Why do people in these areas **live** so long? The answer is lifestyle.[2] This list **shows** six lifestyle habits[3] that **are** common in these places.

1 People in these areas **move** around a lot. They **don't exercise** in a gym, but they **walk** a lot during the day. They **use** their bodies and **live** actively.
2 They **have** a purpose in their lives. Some **spend** time with grandchildren. Others **do** gardening or volunteer work.[4]
3 They **relax**. **Every day**, they **take** time to rest and relax. They **rarely feel** stressed.[5]
4 They **eat** a lot of vegetables, and they **usually don't eat** meat.
5 They **have** many friends. They **are** part of an active social group.
6 They **feel** close to their families.

[1]**researcher:** a person who studies something to learn detailed information about it

[2]**lifestyle:** the way people live; how people eat, sleep, work, exercise

[3]**habit:** something you do or the way you act regularly

[4]**volunteer work:** work without pay, usually to help other people or an organization

[5]**stressed:** very nervous or worried

2 Simple Present: Affirmative and Negative Statements

Grammar Presentation

The simple present describes habits, routines, and facts.	*In some cultures, people live to be 100 years old. These people exercise and eat very well.*

2.1 Affirmative Statements

SINGULAR

Subject	Verb	
I You	**eat**	vegetables every day.
He She It	**eats**	

PLURAL

Subject	Verb	
We You They	**eat**	vegetables every day.

2.2 Negative Statements

SINGULAR

Subject	*Do / Does* + *Not*	Base Form of Verb	
I You	**do not** **don't**	**eat**	a lot of meat.
He She It	**does not** **doesn't**		

PLURAL

Subject	*Do + Not*	Base Form of Verb	
We You They	**do not** **don't**	**exercise**	in the morning.

2.3 Using Simple Present and Time Expressions

A Use simple present to talk about things that regularly happen, such as habits and routines.	*Okinawans usually eat fruits and vegetables.* *We don't eat meat.* *He doesn't drive to work.*

2.3 Using Simple Present and Time Expressions (continued)

B When you talk about things that regularly happen, use time expressions such as *every day*, *every* + day, *in the morning/afternoon/evening*, *at night*, and *at 6:30*.	*They take long walks* every day. *She takes long walks* every Saturday. *We take naps* in the afternoon. *I watch TV* at night. *Our family eats dinner* at 6:30.
An -s after the day of the week/morning/afternoon/evening or weekend means the action or event always happens.	On Saturdays, *I work in a restaurant.* *I take long walks* on weekends.
Use *from . . . to . . .* to say how long something happens.	*I work* from 8:00 to 5:00.
C Time expressions usually come at the end of the sentence. If the time expression is at the beginning of the sentence, use a comma after it.	*I visit my grandparents* in the summer. In the summer, *I visit my grandparents.* In June, *I take a break from school.*
D You can also use the simple present to talk about facts.	*Okinawans* live *long lives.*

2.4 Spelling Rules for Adding -s, -es, and -ies to Verbs

A Add -s to most verbs. Add -s to verbs ending in a vowel[1] + -y.	*drinks, rides, runs, sees, sleeps* *buys, pays, says*
B Add -es to verbs ending in -ch, -sh, -ss, -x. Add -es to verbs ending in a consonant[2] + -o.	*teaches, pushes, misses, fixes* *does, goes*
C For verbs that end in a consonant + -y, change the y to i and add -es.	*cry* → *cries* *study* → *studies*
D Some verbs are irregular.	*be* → *am / are / is* *have* → *has*

Reminder:
[1]**Vowels:** the letters *a, e, i, o, u*
[2]**Consonants:** the letters *b, c, d, f, g, h, j, k, l, m, n, p, q, r, s, t, v, w, x, y, z*
Spelling and Pronunciation Rules for Simple Present: See page A20.

DATA FROM THE REAL WORLD

Here are some of the most frequent simple present verbs:

be	do	get	know	see	come	want
have	say	go	think	make	take	give

⬚ Grammar Application

Complete the sentences with the correct form of the verbs in parentheses.

1 My grandparents __*live*__ (live) healthy lifestyles.

2 My grandfather _____ (go) for a walk every morning.

3 In the afternoon, he _____ (check) his e-mail and _____ (work) in his garden.

4 My grandmother _____ (be) also active.

5 She _____ (work) part-time in a hotel.

6 She _____ (do) volunteer work at a local school three days a week.

7 Before dinner, they _____ (relax) in the living room.

8 They _____ (eat) healthy food, and they _____ (not smoke).

Complete the statements with the affirmative or negative form of the verbs in parentheses.

1 Tran and his roommate, Edgar, __*have*__ (have) a lot to do every week.

2 They often _____ (feel) stressed during the week.

3 Tran _____ (work) long hours at a department store.

4 He _____ (not see) his family very much.

5 Tran and Edgar both _____ (take) night classes at the community college.

6 They usually _____ (not have) time to cook dinner.

7 For dinner, they often _____ (eat) fast food like hamburgers and French fries.

8 Edgar _____ (not have) a job.

9 Every morning, he _____ (go) online to look at job listings.

10 Edgar usually _____ (run) in the afternoon.

11 On the weekends, Edgar and Tran _____ (relax) with friends.

Exercise 2.3 More Simple Present Statements

A Over to You **Complete the sentences about yourself. Use affirmative or negative forms of the verbs in the box.**

do	eat	feel	live	sleep
drink	exercise	have	read	spend

1 I _____ stressed during the week.

2 I _____ good friends in my town.

3 I _____ very actively.

4 I _____ in a gym.

5 I _____ a lot of meat.

6 I _____ about eight hours every night.

7 I _____ a lot of time online or on the computer.

8 I _____ volunteer work in my area.

9 I _____ a lot of water every day.

10 I _____ the news in the morning.

B Pair Work **Share your sentences with a partner. Then change partners. Tell your new partner about your classmate.**

A *Ari feels stressed during the week.*

B *Maria doesn't feel stressed during the week.*

Exercise 2.4 Pronunciation Focus: -s and -es

Say /s/ after /f/, /k/, /p/, and /t/ sounds.	*laughs, drinks, walks, sleeps, writes, gets, texts*
Say /z/ after /b/, /d/, /g/, /v/, /m/, /n/, /l/, and /r/ sounds and all vowel sounds.	*grabs, rides, hugs, lives, comes, runs, smiles, hears, sees, plays, buys, goes, studies*
Say /əz/ after /tʃ/, /ʃ/, /s/, /ks/, /z/, and /dʒ/ sounds.	*teaches, pushes, kisses, fixes, uses, changes*
Pronounce the vowel sound in *does* and *says* differently from *do* and *say*.	*do* /du:/ → *does* /dʌz/ *say* /seɪ/ → *says* /sez/

A Listen and repeat the verbs in the chart above.

B Read about Staci's week. Underline the verbs that end in *-s* or *-es*.

Staci <u>goes</u> to school from Monday to Friday from 7:30 a.m. to 11:30 a.m. Then she rushes to work. She works at a hospital until 8:00 p.m. In the evening, Staci catches a bus to go home. On her way home, she listens to music and relaxes. She eats a quick dinner with her family. Then she reads to her children and checks their homework. If she isn't too tired, she finishes her own homework. Staci usually falls asleep by 10:00 p.m.

C Listen to the information about Staci's week and check (✓) the sounds of the verbs in the boxes below. Then practice saying the verbs.

	/s/	/z/	/əz/
1 goes		✓	
2 rushes			
3 works			
4 catches			
5 listens			
6 relaxes			
7 eats			
8 reads			
9 checks			
10 finishes			
11 falls			

D Pair Work Ask and answer the questions with a partner. Then tell the class about your partner.

1 What are two of your healthy habits?

2 What do you do to relax?

Paulo eats healthy food, and he doesn't smoke or drink. To relax, he listens to music.

Exercise 2.5 Using Time Expressions with Simple Present

Allie's Schedule

	Sunday	Monday	Tuesday	Wednesday	Thursday	Friday	Saturday
Morning	Off	Get up 6:30 a.m. Work 7:30 a.m.–2:30 p.m.	Get up 6:30 a.m. Work 7:30 a.m.–2:30 p.m.	Get up 6:30 a.m. Work 7:30 a.m.–2:30 p.m.	Get up 6:30 a.m. Work 7:30 a.m.–2:30 p.m.	Get up 6:30 a.m. Work 7:30 a.m.–2:30 p.m.	Off
Afternoon	Visit parents	Yoga		Yoga			Do homework
Evening			Class 7:15–9:45 p.m.		Class 7:15–9:45 p.m.		
	Bed at 11:00 p.m.	Bed at 11:00 p.m.	Bed at 11:00 p.m.	Bed at 11:00 p.m.	Bed at 11:00 p.m.	Bed at 11:00 p.m.	

A Look at Allie's schedule and complete the sentences about it. Use the correct time expressions.

Time	**Part of Day / Day of Week**
at (time)	*in the* (morning / afternoon / evening)
from (time) *to* (time)	*on* (day of week)

Use *at* (time) and *from* (time / day) *to* (time / day) to indicate exact times and days.

Use *on* (day of week) or *in the* (morning / afternoon / evening) to indicate the day or part of day.

1 Allie goes to yoga _on Mondays and Wednesdays_ . (days)

2 She works _from Monday to Friday_ . (days)

3 She works _____ . (times)

4 She has classes _____ . (days)

5 Her classes are _____ . (times)

6 Her days off are _____ . (days)

7 She visits her parents _____ . (day)

8 During the week, she usually goes to bed _____ and

wakes up _____ . (times)

9 She does her homework _____ . (day)

B Over to You Think about your schedule. Complete the sentences below. Make them true for you.

1 I take classes (days) _on Mondays, Tuesdays, Wednesdays, and Thursdays_ .

2 My classes are (time) _____ .

3 I work (days) _____ .

4 I work (time) _____ .

5 During the week, I go to sleep (time) _____ .

6 On the weekends, I go to sleep (time) _____ .

7 On Sundays, I get up (time) _____ .

8 I do my homework (time) _____ .

3 Statements with Adverbs of Frequency

Grammar Presentation

Adverbs of frequency describe how often something happens.	*Our neighbors never drive to work. They always ride their bikes.*

3.1 Adverbs of Frequency

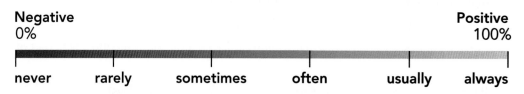

Negative 0%   **Positive** 100%

never   rarely   sometimes   often   usually   always

Rarely is not frequently used.

3.2 Adverbs of Frequency

Subject	Adverb of Frequency	Verb	
I You We They	always usually often sometimes	work	10 hours a day.
He She It	rarely never	works	

Adverbs of Frequency with *Be*

Subject	*Be*	Adverb of Frequency	
I	am		
You We They	are	always usually often sometimes rarely never	tired.
He She It	is		

3.3 Using Adverbs of Frequency

A Adverbs of frequency usually come after the verb *be*.	*I am often busy in the afternoon.* *She is usually tired in the morning.*
B Adverbs of frequency usually come before other verbs.	*My parents rarely eat meat.* *Cristina often rides her bike to work.* *He doesn't usually watch TV.*
C *Sometimes, usually,* and *often* can come before the verb OR at the beginning or end of a sentence.	*We sometimes cook for our family.* *Sometimes we cook for our family.* *We cook for our family sometimes.*
D Do not begin or end sentences with *always* and *never*.	*Your grandparents are always active.* NOT ~~Always~~ *your grandparents are active.* NOT *Your grandparents are active* ~~never~~*.*

Grammar Application

Exercise 3.1 Adverbs of Frequency with Simple Present

Unscramble the words to make sentences.

1 happy / My / always / is / brother / at work.
   My brother is always happy at work.

2 music. / He / listen to / does / not / often

   _____

3 slows down. / never / He

   _____

4 sometimes / He / seven / works / a week. / days

   _____

5 takes / He / a day off. / rarely

   _____

6 starts / in / work / He / at 3:00 / usually / the afternoon.

   _____

7 until 1:00 a.m. / doesn't / He / usually / finish

   _____

8 is / tired. / rarely / My brother

   _____

A Over to You **Read the sentences and check (✓) the boxes. Make them true for you.**

Talk About Your Lifestyle

	NEVER	SOMETIMES	OFTEN	USUALLY	ALWAYS
1 I get eight hours of sleep at night.					
2 I fall asleep easily.					
3 I wake up at night.					
4 I exercise three times a week.					
5 I have dinner with friends on the weekend.					
6 I watch TV at night.					
7 I go to the library one day a month.					
8 I go away for vacation.					

B Pair Work **Take turns saying your sentences from A with a partner.**

A *I never get eight hours of sleep at night. How about you, Olga?*

B *I sometimes get eight hours of sleep at night.*

4 Avoid Common Mistakes

1 **For affirmative statements with *he/she/it*, use the base form of the verb + *-s* / *-es*.**

relaxes
He ~~relax~~ after lunch.

2 **For affirmative statements with *I/you/we/they* or a plural noun, use the base form of the verb.**

go
My parents ~~goes~~ out to dinner every Friday night.

3 **In negative statements, use *do not* / *don't* or *does not* / *doesn't* + the base form of the verb.**

jog
Maria does not ~~jogs~~ after dark.

4 **Do not use *do* or *does* in negative statements with *be*.**

am not
I ~~don't be~~ active on social media.

5 **Do not use *be* with a simple present verb.**
I am exercise on Tuesdays.

Editing Task

Find and correct 10 more mistakes in the letter.

Dear Pedro,

live

How are you? I'm fine. I'm in Vermont with my aunt and uncle. They ~~lives~~

on a farm. The lifestyle here is very different. They are dairy farmers, so they

are work hard every day. They usually get up at 4:30 a.m. They go to the barn

5   and milk the cows. Cows makes a lot of noise in the morning, so they usually

wakes me up. Of course, I do not gets up until about 7:00 a.m. At 9:00, my

uncle cook a wonderful breakfast. We all eat together. After that, he and I

goes to the barn and works there. My aunt usually stay in the house. In the

afternoon, there is more work. At night, I am really tired, so I always goes to

10   bed at 8:30! Usually my aunt and uncle don't be tired. They usually go to bed

late!

I hope your vacation is fun. See you soon!

Your friend,

Oscar

5 Academic Writing

Writing about Daily Life

Brainstorm ⟩ Organize ⟩ Write ⟩ Edit

In this writing cycle (Units 8-10), you are going to answer the prompt below. In this unit (8), you will read about a student's daily life and then use a schedule to brainstorm ideas.

Write about the life of a classmate.

Exercise 5.1 Preparing to Write

List things you do on weekdays and on the weekend. Compare your list with a partner.

weekdays	weekend

Exercise 5.2 Focusing on Vocabulary

Read the sentences. Choose the correct definition for the words in bold.

1 After lunch, I like to take a nap in the **afternoon**.
   a a time between 12 p.m. and 5 p.m.   b a place you sleep

2 I am very **busy** with school. I take many classes.
   a having a lot of friends   b having a lot of things to do

3 My **schedule** is the same every day. I work and then go to school.
   a a place where you work to make money   b a list of planned activities or things to do

4 I get up at 6:00 every **morning**. I make coffee and eat breakfast.
   a a time between 5 a.m. and noon   b the place where you make food

5 I **relax** after work. I watch TV.
   a to become calm and comfortable   b to do many things

6 In the **evening**, I do my homework and read a book before bed.
   a the place where you go to relax   b a time between 5 p.m. and 11 p.m.

7 I have school on **weekdays**. I always have to get up early.
   a Monday to Friday, when many people work
   b Saturday and Sunday, when many people do not work

8 On the **weekend**, I usually ride my bike. I have fun with friends.
   a Saturday and Sunday, when many people do not work
   b Monday to Friday, when many people work

Matteo's Daily Schedule

1 Matteo Taha is a college student. He has a **busy schedule**. Matteo studies engineering at the University of Michigan. He takes five classes. They are physics, calculus, English, engineering, and history. His favorite classes are physics and calculus.

2 Matteo has three classes every **weekday morning**. He gets up at 6 a.m. every day. Then he has physics from 8 a.m. to 9 a. m., calculus from 9:15 a.m. to 10:15 a.m., and engineering from 10:30 a.m. to 11:30 a.m.

3 On Monday and Wednesday **afternoons**, he has English. His English class is from 2 p.m. to 3 p.m. On Thursday afternoons, he has history from 2 p.m. to 3 p.m. On Friday afternoons, he meets with his study group. His study group is from 12:30 p.m. to 1:30 p.m. In the **evenings**, Matteo often studies in the library.

4 On the **weekend**, Matteo usually **relaxes** with friends. Sometimes he goes to the pool to swim. He enjoys his busy life.

Name of student: _Matteo Taha_   **Major:** _Engineering_

morning							
	Sun.	**Mon.**	**Tue.**	**Wed.**	**Thur.**	**Fri.**	**Sat.**
8-9 a.m.		Physics 101	Physics 101	Physics 101	Physics 101	Physics 101	
9:15-10:15 a.m.		Calculus 121	Calculus 121	Calculus 121	Calculus 121	Calculus 121	
10:30-11:30 a.m.		Engineering 122	Engineering 122	Engineering 122	Engineering 122	Engineering 122	

afternoon							
	Sun.	**Mon.**	**Tue.**	**Wed.**	**Thur.**	**Fri.**	**Sat.**
12:30-1:30 p.m.						Study group	
2-3 p.m.		English 101	Library	English 101	History 123		

evening							
	Sun.	**Mon.**	**Tue.**	**Wed.**	**Thur.**	**Fri.**	**Sat.**
5-7 p.m.	Relax with friends	Library	Library	Library		Library	
7-10 p.m.	Relax with friends	Library		Go to the gym		Library	

Read the text on page 111. Work with a partner. Ask and answer the questions.

1 What is Matteo's last name? _____

2 What college does Matteo go to? _____

3 What classes does he take? _____

4 When does he get up? _____

5 When are his classes? _____

6 When does he meet with his study group? _____

7 When does he go to the library? _____

8 When does he relax with friends? _____

Exercise 5.4 Noticing the Grammar and Structure

Complete the tasks. When you finish, compare your answers with a partner's.

1 Underline the verbs in paragraph 1. What tense does the writer use? Why?

_____

_____

2 Highlight the sentence in paragraph 1 that states the paragraph's main idea. Write the main idea.

_____

_____

3 Circle the words and phrases the writer uses in paragraph 3 to show time relationships. Write them below.

_____

_____

4 Put a box around three adverbs of frequency. Write them in the blanks.

_____   _____   _____

My Writing

Exercise 5.5 Brainstorming

Work with a partner. Ask and answer questions like the ones in Exercise 5.3 about your daily lives. Write your partner's answers in the schedule.

Name of student:			Major:				
morning							
Times	Sun.	Mon.	Tue.	Wed.	Thur.	Fri.	Sat.
afternoon							
Times	Sun.	Mon.	Tue.	Wed.	Thur.	Fri.	Sat.
evening							
Times	Sun.	Mon.	Tue.	Wed.	Thur.	Fri.	Sat.

Simple Present Yes/No Questions and Short Answers

Daily Habits

1 Grammar in the Real World

A Do you get enough sleep? Do you have trouble sleeping? Read the news article about sleeping habits. Answer the survey questions.

B Comprehension Check Circle the correct answer.

1 This article is about **health/sleep** habits.

2 Sleep is a **problem/hobby** for many people.

3 Many people believe poor sleep can affect their **work/friends**.

C Notice Find the questions in the news article, and choose the correct word to complete the questions. Then underline the subject of each sentence.

1 **Do/Does** most adults think sleep is important?

2 **Do/Does** productivity improve after a good night's sleep?

3 **Do/Does** you feel good about your sleep habits?

Notice the use of *do* and *does*. Which word do you use for singular subjects? Which word do you use for plural subjects?

Do most people get
ENOUGH SLEEP?

If you think "no," you are correct. The National Sleep Foundation's 2010 Sleep in America™ poll[1] shows that sleep is a problem for many people. About 75 percent agree that poor sleep can affect their work or family relationships. How are your sleep habits? To find out, answer the
5 survey[2] questions below.

[1]**poll:** a short questionnaire, usually one question

[2]**survey:** a set of questions to find out people's habits or beliefs about something

[3]**suffer from insomnia:** find it difficult to get to sleep or to sleep well

		Yes	No
---	---	:-::	:-:
1	**Do** you **fall asleep** in 30 minutes or less?	❑	❑
2	**Do** you **have** trouble falling asleep?	❑	❑
3	**Do** you **suffer** from insomnia?[3]	❑	❑
4	**Does** stress **keep** you awake?	❑	❑
10 5	**Do** you **take** any sleep medication?	❑	❑
6	**Do** you **wake up** during the night?	❑	❑
7	**Do** you **wake up** too early in the morning?	❑	❑
8	**Do** you **feel** very tired in the morning?	❑	❑
9	**Do** you **get** at least seven hours of sleep each night?	❑	❑
15 10	**Do** you **get** more sleep on the weekends?	❑	❑

2 Simple Present *Yes/No* Questions and Short Answers

Grammar Presentation

You can use simple present questions to ask about habits, routines, and facts.	*Do you wake up early?* *Does she suffer from insomnia?*

2.1 *Yes/No* Questions

Do / Does	Subject	Base Form of Verb	
Do	I you we they	**fall asleep**	in 30 minutes?
Does	he she it		

2.2 Short Answers

AFFIRMATIVE

Yes	Subject	Do / Does
Yes,	I you we they	**do.**
	he she it	**does.**

NEGATIVE

No	Subject	Do / Does + Not
No,	I You We They	**do not.** **don't.**
	he she it	**does not.** **doesn't.**

2.3 Using Simple Present *Yes/No* Questions and Answers

A For simple present *Yes/No* questions, use *Do* or *Does* with the base form of the verb.	*Do you feel tired every morning?* *Does he wake up during the night?*
B People usually use contractions in negative short answers.	"*Do you watch TV all night?*" "*No, I don't.*"
Be careful! Negative full forms are very strong. You can sound angry.	"*No, I do not!*" (This can sound angry.)

2.3 Using Simple Present *Yes / No* Questions and Answers *(continued)*

C You can give longer answers to *Yes / No* questions. It's friendly to give more information.	*"Do you fall asleep easily?"* *"Yes, I usually fall asleep in about 15 minutes."* *"No, I often stay awake for an hour."*
You can also give a short answer and then give more information in a separate sentence.	*"Yes, I do. I usually fall asleep in about 15 minutes."* *"No, I don't. I often stay awake for an hour."*
D Some questions do not have a simple *yes* or *no* answer. You can answer *Well, . . .* and give a longer answer in speaking.	*"Do you live with your family?"* *"Well, I live with my aunt and uncle."*
Do not use *Well, . . .* to answer questions in academic writing, for example in compositions or tests.	*"Does the average college student get a lot of sleep?"* *"The average student gets about six hours of sleep."* NOT *"Well, the average student gets about six hours of sleep."*

Grammar Application

Exercise 2.1 *Yes / No* Questions and Short Answers

A Complete the questions with *Do* or *Does*. Then write short answers. Make them true for you.

1 ___*Do*___ you get up early?   _Yes, I do. / No, I don't._

2 _____ the sun wake you up?   _____

3 _____ your alarm play music?   _____

4 _____ you often go back to sleep?   _____

5 _____ you like mornings?   _____

6 _____ you sleep until noon on the weekends?   _____

7 _____ you usually stay up past midnight?   _____

8 _____ you study late at night?   _____

B Pair Work   Ask and answer the questions in A. Give short answers to your partner's questions.

A *Do you get up early?*

B *No, I don't.*

A Complete the conversation about other habits. Write questions with the words in parentheses. Then complete the short answers.

Lucy	*Do you and your brother share* _____
	(1)
	(you and your brother/share) the cooking?
Malia	No, _____ . I'm always busy with school.
	(2)
Lucy	So, _____
	(3)
	(your brother/do) all the cooking?
Malia	Yes, _____ . He's a great cook.
	(4)
Lucy	_____ (he/work)
	(5)
	in a restaurant?
Malia	No, _____ .
	(6)
Lucy	Oh, _____
	(7)
	(he/go) to cooking school?
Malia	No, _____ . He just loves food.
	(8)

B Pair Work Practice the conversations in A with a partner.

> In speaking, people often say *Do you* very fast.
> It can sound like one word ("D'you").
> Always write *Do you* as two words, but say it fast so it sounds like one word ("D'you").

A Listen to the questions about people's music habits. Repeat the questions. Say *Do you* fast, as one word.

Do you fall asleep with music on?   Do you study with music on?

Do you like loud music?   Do you sing along to music?

Do you dance when you listen to music?   Do you have a television in your bedroom?

Do you listen to music all the time?

B Pair Work Ask and answer the questions in A. Give a short answer first, and then give more information in a second sentence. Use *Well, . . .* for some answers.

  A *Do you like loud music?*   **A** *Do you listen to music all the time?*

  B *No, I don't. I prefer soft music.*   **B** *Well, I don't listen to music when I'm in class.*

Exercise 2.4 *Yes/No Questions in a Survey*

A Over to You Write questions for these habits. Then ask your classmates these questions. Write their names in the chart.

Who . . . ?			Name
falls asleep with the TV on	1	*Do you fall asleep with the TV on?*	
falls asleep to music	2		
talks in his or her sleep	3		
dreams a lot	4		
remembers his or her dreams	5		
walks in his or her sleep	6		

B Pair Work Tell a partner about four classmates and their sleeping habits.

Delia talks in her sleep.

3 Avoid Common Mistakes ⚠

1 **Use *Do* with plural subjects and with *you*.**

    Do
~~Does~~ your roommates stay up late?

2 **Use *Does* with singular subjects (except *you*).**

Does
~~Do~~ this this coffee maker have a timer?

3 **Use *Do / Does* in simple present questions with *have*.**

Do you have
~~Have you~~ a website?

4 **Do not use *Do / Does* in questions with *be*.**

Is
~~Do~~ your phone new?

5 **Do not use *Be* with other simple present verbs.**

Do
~~Are~~ you agree?

Editing Task

Find and correct seven more mistakes in these questions about sleeping habits.

  Do you have
1 ~~Have you~~ trouble falling asleep?

2 Are you sleep on your stomach, your back, or your side?

3 Have you a TV in your bedroom?

4 Does you dream in color or in black-and-white?

5 Do a dream ever scare you?

6 Does loud noises wake you up at night?

7 Do you a light sleeper or a deep sleeper?

8 Does you fall asleep quickly?

4 Academic Writing

Writing about a Lifestyle

Brainstorm > **Organize** > Write > Edit

In Unit 8, you started brainstorming ideas to answer the prompt below. In this unit (9), you will learn about main ideas and details and then use a chart to find and start organizing details for your paragraph.

> Write about the life of a classmate.

Main Ideas and Details

A **main idea** states what a paragraph is about. It is often at the beginning of the paragraph. The write then adds **details** to give more information and explain the main idea.

Matteo Taha (is a college student). He has a busy schedule. Matteo studies engineering at the University of Michigan. He takes five classes. They are physics, calculus, English, engineering, and history. His favorite classes are physics and calculus.

The main idea in the example is: Matteo Taha **is a college student**. The details give more information about Matteo's life as a student. The supporting sentences talk about his schedule, school, and classes.

Exercise 4.1 Applying the Skill

1 Read the paragraph below. Circle the main idea and underline the details.

> Matteo is very busy on weekday mornings. He gets up at 6 a.m. every day and drives to college. Then he has physics from 8 a.m. to 9 a.m., calculus from 9:15 a.m. to 10:15 a.m., and engineering from 10:30 a.m. to 11:30 a.m.

2 Work with a partner. Ask and answer the questions.
 a What classes does Matteo have in the morning?
 b What details are there about his morning classes?

c Are there any details about his afternoon classes? Why or why not?

d What detail could the writer include in this paragraph?

- Matteo meets with his study group on Friday afternoon.
- Matteo has breakfast at 7 a.m.
- Matteo has English on Monday and Wednesday afternoon.

3 Read the paragraph below. Circle the main idea and underline the details. Then add one more sentence to give another detail. Use your own ideas.

> On the weekend, Matteo usually relaxes with friends. Sometimes he goes to the pool to swim. _____ He enjoys his busy life.

My Writing

Exercise 4.2 Finding Details

Ask questions to find more details about your partner's life for your paragraph. Make notes in the chart.

	Details
What subjects does he/she study?	
What is his/her favorite subject?	
When does he/she get up?	
What is his/her school schedule?	
What does he/she do on the weekends?	
How does he/she feel about this schedule?	

Exercise 4.3 Adding Information

Work with your partner. Ask and answer the questions. Add any important new details to your notes for your paragraph.

1 Do you feel tired in the morning? _____

2 Do you take classes in the morning? _____

3 Do you take classes in the afternoon? _____

4 Do you study with friends? _____

5 Do you study in the library? _____

6 Do you study late at night? _____

7 Do you relax on the weekends? _____

8 Do you enjoy your life as a student? _____

10 Simple Present Information Questions

Cultural Holidays

1 Grammar in the Real World

A What is your favorite holiday or celebration? Read the interview about a Mexican holiday. What is the Day of the Dead?

B Comprehension Check **Choose the correct answers.**

1 On the Day of the Dead, people remember _____ .
   a their parents   b their dead relatives   c their children

2 People put pictures of the dead _____ .
   a on altars   b on sweets   c on skulls

3 The Day of the Dead takes place _____ .
   a every month   b one day a year   c on November 1 and 2

4 People _____ their ancestors' graves.
   a decorate   b paint   c celebrate

C Notice **Answer the questions with the correct question word. Use the interview to help you.**

1 Which word asks a question about **time**?   What   When   Where

2 Which word asks a question about **places**?   What   When   Where

3 Which word asks a question about **things**?   What   When   Where

What word comes after *when*, *where*, and *what*?

Coffee Time

Today's Topic:
MEXICO'S DAY of the DEAD

[1]**ancestor:** any member of your family from long ago

[2]**altar:** a type of table that people use in religious ceremonies

[3]**grave:** a place where you bury a dead person or people, usually under the ground

[4]**skull:** the bones of the head around the brain

[5]**symbolize:** use a sign or mark to represent something

[6]**rebirth:** a new period of growth of something

Michelle Hello, everyone! This is *Coffee Time*. Our topic today is celebrations around the world. Today our guest is Elena Lopez, from a university in Mexico. She's here to tell us about the Day of the Dead. Welcome, Dr. Lopez!

5 **Dr. Lopez** Thank you. It's nice to be here.

Michelle First of all, **where do people celebrate the Day of the Dead?**

Dr. Lopez They celebrate it in many parts of the world, such as in Mexico.

10 **Michelle** **When do people celebrate it, and how do they celebrate it?**

Dr. Lopez Well, the Day of the Dead takes place on two days: November 1 and 2. We remember our dead relatives – our ancestors[1] – and friends. People build little altars[2] 15 in the home and in public schools. They also clean and decorate the graves.[3]

Michelle **What do they put on these altars and graves?**

Dr. Lopez They put candles, food, drinks, flowers, and pictures of the dead. There are sweets in the shape of skulls,[4] too. 20 The traditions are a little different in every region of Mexico.

Michelle **What do the different things mean?**

Dr. Lopez Well, for example, the candles are a guide for our ancestors. They guide them home. There are bells, too. 25 They call the dead.

Michelle **What do the skulls symbolize?**[5] Do they symbolize death?

Dr. Lopez Well, yes. But they also symbolize rebirth,[6] according to the first Day of the Dead thousands of years ago.

Cultural Holidays 123

2 Simple Present Information Questions

Grammar Presentation

Information questions begin with a *Wh-* word (*Who, What, When, Where, Why,* or *How*). They ask for information and cannot be answered with a simple *yes* or *no*.

Where do people celebrate the Day of the Dead?

When do Americans celebrate Independence Day?

2.1 Information Questions

Wh- word	Do / Does	Subject	Base Form of Verb	
Who	do	I you we they	see	at school?
What			eat	at parties?
When			celebrate	that holiday?
What time			begin	the celebration?
Where	does	he she it	study	for school?
Why			live	at home?
How			meet	new people?

2.2 Using Simple Present Information Questions

A Use a *Wh-* word with *do* before *I, you, we, they,* and plural nouns.	*When do you celebrate the holiday?*	
Use a *Wh-* word with *does* before *he, she, it,* and singular nouns.	*Why does she study Spanish?*	
B Use simple present information questions to ask for specific information.	*"Where do you live?"* *"I live in Mexico City."* *"What time do you start work?"* *"8:30."*	
C Use simple present information questions to ask about habits, facts, traditions, and regular activities.	*"When do they celebrate the Day of the Dead?"* *"In November."* *"Why does she travel to Mexico every year?"* *"Because she has family there."*	
D You can answer information questions with a short or long answer.	*"What do you eat on Thanksgiving?"* Short answer: *"Turkey and pie."* Long answer: *"I eat turkey and pie."*	

2.3 Using *Wh-* Words

A Use *Who* to ask about people.	*"Who do you remember on the Day of the Dead?"* *"I remember my grandmother."*
B Use *What* to ask about things.	*"What do you study?"* *"Spanish and history."*
C Use *When* to ask about time (days, months, years, seasons, parts of the day).	*"When do you celebrate Chinese New Year?"* *"In January or February."*
D Use *What time* to ask about clock time.	*"What time does your class finish?"* *"4:30. / Five o'clock."*
E Use *Where* to ask about places.	*"Where does she work?"* *"At the University of Mexico."*
F Use *Why* to ask about reasons.	*"Why do you like celebrations?"* *"Because they're always fun."*
G Use *How* to ask about manner – the way people do something.	*"How do you celebrate your birthday?"* *"We eat at my favorite restaurant."*

Grammar Application

Exercise 2.1 Questions with *Who, What, When, Where, How*

A Complete the questions with *Who, What, When, Where,* or *How* and *do* or *does.*

1 **A** _Where_ _do_ people celebrate the Day of the Dead?
   B In Mexico.

2 **A** _____ _____ they celebrate the Day of the Dead?
   B On November 1 and 2.

3 **A** _____ _____ they remember?
   B Their dead relatives and friends.

4 **A** _____ _____ they decorate?
   B Graves and altars.

5 **A** _____ _____ they put pictures of the dead?
   B On altars.

6 **A** _____ _____ they decorate the graves?
   B With flowers, candles, food, and drinks.

B Over to You Unscramble the words and add *do* or *does* to make questions. Then write answers that are true for you.

1 what celebration / you / like / the best / ?

A *What celebration do you like the best?*

B _____

2 when / you / celebrate / it / ?

A _____

B _____

3 who / you / celebrate / it / with / ?

A _____

B _____

4 what / you / usually / do / ?

A _____

B _____

5 where / you / celebrate / it / ?

A _____

B _____

6 what / you / usually / eat / ?

A _____

B _____

7 when / it / usually / end / ?

A _____

B _____

C Pair Work Ask and answer the questions in B with a partner.

Exercise 2.2 Questions with *When* and *What Time*

A Complete the questions with *When* or *What time* and *do* or *does*.

1 A <u>When</u> <u>do</u> you graduate?   B On June 15.

2 A _____ _____ you have the ceremony?   B At 3:30.

3 A _____ _____ Sandi turn 21?   B Next Saturday.

4 A _____ _____ her birthday party start?   B At 7:00.

5 A _____ _____ you celebrate Thanksgiving in the B At the end of November.
   United States?

6 A _____ _____ your family usually have the meal? B In the late afternoon.

7 A _____ _____ you usually start cooking on that day? B At about 8:00 a.m.

B Pair Work Ask and answer the questions in A with a partner.

Exercise 2.3 Asking Information Questions

A Read the paragraph about a holiday celebration in Massachusetts. Write information questions using the words in parentheses. Find the verbs in the paragraph, and use the information to write your questions. Remember to use *do* and *does* in your questions.

One of my favorite holidays is Patriots' Day in the Boston, Massachusetts, area. Every year, Boston residents celebrate Patriots' Day on the third Monday of April. On this day, people remember the beginning of the American Revolutionary War. Many towns have parades and speeches.[1] The second important event is the Boston Marathon.[2] The marathon happens every year on Patriots' Day. The race starts around 10:00 a.m. in Hopkinton and ends in Boston. Thousands of people watch runners from all over the world. The third event is the special Patriots' Day baseball game. The Boston Red Sox play a team from another town. The game starts around 11:00 a.m. in Boston.

[1]speech: a formal talk | **[2]marathon:** a race in which people run 26 miles and 385 yards (42.195 kilometers)

1 (what / people / celebrate) <u>What do people celebrate on the third Monday of April?</u>

2 (what / people / remember) _____

3 (what / towns / have) _____

4 (when / marathon / happen) _____

5 (what time / marathon / start) _____

6 (where / marathon / start) _____

7 (who / people / watch) _____

B Pair Work **Ask and answer the questions in A with a partner.**

> **A** *What do people celebrate on the third Monday of April?*
> **B** *They celebrate Patriots' Day.*

Exercise 2.4 Pronunciation Focus: Intonation in Questions

In information questions, our voice usually *goes down*. We call this falling intonation.	Where do you go on va**ca**tion? Why do you stay **home**? When do you see your **re**latives?
In *Yes/No* questions, our voice often *goes up*. We call this rising intonation.	Do you celebrate Me**mo**rial Day? Is that your favorite day of the **year**? Does she work at **night**?

A **Listen to the questions and answers. Mark the questions with ↗ for rising intonation and ↘ for falling intonation.**

1. **A** Excuse me. Are you from Japan? ↗
   B Yes, I am. I'm from Tokyo.

2. **A** Can I ask you some questions? _____
   B Sure!

3. **A** What's your favorite holiday in Japan? _____
   B New Year's Day.

4. **A** Why is it your favorite? _____
   B Because we have special food for the holiday, and we relax all day.

5. **A** Do you help your mother with the cooking? _____
   B Yes, I do. We also see all our relatives on New Year's Day.

6. **A** Do you play any special games? _____
   B No, not really. But we watch some special TV programs.

7. **A** What else do you do on New Year's Day? _____
   B Well, we read all our holiday cards then.

8. **A** Do you really save all the cards to open on the same day? _____
   B Yes, it's a special custom.

B **Listen and repeat the questions.**

Exercise 2.5 Information Questions in Titles

DATA FROM THE REAL WORLD

We often use information questions in the titles of academic articles and books. The article or book answers the question.

Titles with *How? What?* and *Why?* are very frequent.

Why Do We Laugh?
How Does a Computer Work?
When Do People Watch TV?

A Read the quotations from academic articles. Choose a title for each article from the box.

Why Do People Celebrate Holidays?	What Do Teens Search for on the Internet?
How Do People Make New Friends?	Why Does a Bird Learn to Sing?
When Does a Child Become an Adult?	~~What Do Children Like to Eat?~~
Why Do We Dream?	Why Do We Grow Old?

1 *What Do Children Like to Eat?*
"Children prefer food that is not very hot or very strong in flavor."

2 _____
"Birds need to communicate with other birds."

3 _____
"We need to bring people together to remember good and bad events in our cultures."

4 _____
"Our body is a machine. It works hard every day, year after year."

5 _____
"Most searches are about movie stars, singers, and sports personalities."

6 _____
"We make friends with people we have something in common with, often at work or school."

7 _____
"We dream because our minds need to rest."

8 _____
"Teenagers are young adults, and the years 16 to 18 are very important."

B Over to You Do you know more about the topics in A? Tell a partner.

A lot of children don't like spicy food.

3 Questions with *How Often*

Grammar Presentation

Questions with *How often* ask about how many times something happens.	*How often does she travel to Mexico?* *How often do you see your family?*

3.1 Questions with *How Often*

How Often	Do/Does	Subject	Base Form of Verb	
How often	**do**	I/you/we/they	**take**	a vacation?
	does	he/she/it	**receive**	a gift?

3.2 Using Questions with *How Often*

A Use questions with *How often* to ask how many times something happens.	*How often do you run in a marathon?* *How often does your family eat together?*
B The answers are often frequency expressions.	*All the time.* *Every day.* *Every weekend.* *Every other week.* *Once a week.* *Twice a month.* *Three times a month.* *Several times a year.* *A few times a year.* *Once in a while.* *Almost never.*

Grammar Application

Exercise 3.1 Questions with *How Often*

A Use the words to write questions with *How often*. Write true answers. Then ask and answer questions with a partner.

1 you/drink coffee

Question: *How often do you drink coffee?*

Answer: *Every day.*

2 you/drink soda

Question: _____

Answer: _____

3 you/eat breakfast alone

Question: _____

Answer: _____

4 your family / go out to a nice restaurant

Question: _____

Answer: _____

5 your friends / eat at a fast-food restaurant

Question: _____

Answer: _____

6 your relatives / visit your home

Question: _____

Answer: _____

B Over to You **Use *How often* to write your own questions on a separate piece of paper. Use words from the box and your own ideas. Then ask your partner the questions.**

board game	hiking	movie	swimming	TV
gym	library	music concert	text message	

How often do you watch TV past midnight?

4 Avoid Common Mistakes ⚠

1 **In simple present information questions, use *do* or *does* before the subject.**

    do   *does*
Where ⌄you work?   Why ⌄he drink so much coffee?

2 **Use *do* or *does*, not *is* or *are*, with the verb.**

              does
What time ~~is~~ the concert begin?

3 **Do not use -*s* on the verb with *he* / *she* / *it* or a singular noun.**

                  go
Where does Tom ~~goes~~ to school?

Editing Task

Find and correct seven more mistakes in these questions about Thanksgiving.

    do
1 How⌄you celebrate Thanksgiving?

2 Where do you celebrates Thanksgiving?

3 What are you does during Thanksgiving Day?

4 What you watch on TV?

5 What time are you usually have your meal?

6 What you do on the Friday after Thanksgiving?

7 Why people celebrate Thanksgiving?

5 Academic Writing

Writing about Daily Life

Brainstorm > Organize > **Write** > **Edit**

In Unit 9, you learned about main ideas and details and then organized ideas to answer the prompt below. In this unit (10), you will write, revise, and edit your paragraph.

> *Write about the life of a classmate.*

My Writing

Exercise 5.1 Writing Your Paragraph

1 Review your work in My Writing in Units 8 and 9.

2 Write the topic sentence:

_____ (*partner's name*) is a student in my _____ (*subject*) class.

This is *his/her* schedule.

3 Write the supporting sentences:
- Write sentences about your partner's schedule.
- Write a sentence about the subject(s) he/she studies.
- Write a sentence about his/her favorite subject.
- Write a sentence about the time he/she gets up.
- Write three sentences about his/her school or university schedule.
- Write one sentence about his/her weekend or free time
- Write one sentence about how he/she feels about the schedule.

Adding Details about Time and Place

Specific details about time and place make an essay more interesting. When you write about a person's daily life, use *When* and *Where* questions to brainstorm more details about your ideas.

When do you go to the library? ➜ I go to the library **in the evenings**.

When do you take biology class ➜ I take biology class **on Mondays and Wednesdays**.

Where do you study with your friends? ➜ I study with my friends **in the student lounge**.

Where do you go on the weekends? ➜ I go **to the movies** on the weekends.

Exercise 5.2 Applying the Skill

Work with your partner. Ask *When?* and *Where?* questions like the ones in the skill box to help you add details about your partner's life to your paragraph.

Exercise 5.3 Revising Your Ideas

1 Work with a partner. Use the questions below to give feedback on your partner's paragraph.

- Which details in your partner's paragraph are the most interesting?
- Which details in your partner's paragraph are unnecessary?
- What details could your partner add to make the paragraph better?

2 Use the feedback from your partner to revise your paragraph.

Exercise 5.4 Editing Your Writing

Use the checklist to review and edit your paragraph.

Did you write a topic sentence with the main idea?	
Did you write supporting sentences that add details?	
Did you use the simple present to talk about routines, habits, and facts?	
Did you spell simple present third-person verbs correctly?	
Did you use adverbs of frequency to make your writing accurate?	
Did you put the adverbs of frequency in the correct place?	

1 Grammar in the Real World

A Do you have enough time for school, work, and family? Read the article. What is one way to manage your time well?

B Comprehension Check **Answer the questions. Use the article to help you.**

1 What do most adults not have enough of?

2 What are two ways to manage your time?

3 What happens when people make plans and complete them?

C Notice **Find the words *and, but, or,* and *because* in the article. Then complete the sentences.**

1 They are busy with work, family, _____ school.

2 People feel stressed _____ there is not enough time to do it all.

3 Some people don't like schedules, lists, _____ weekly plans.

4 Put a reminder for the task on your phone, _____ don't forget to do it!

TIME FOR EVERYTHING

Many adults say they want more time. They are busy with work, family, **and** school, **and** they often don't get everything done. People feel stressed **because** there is not enough time to do it all. However, there are some simple ways to manage your time well **and** avoid stress.

5 One way is to identify the important **or** necessary tasks for that day. Then create a schedule **or** a "to do" list.¹ When you finish your important tasks, you can move on to the next, less important ones. Soon your tasks are done, **and** there is hopefully some extra time for fun activities.

Another way is to do important tasks on the same days every week.
10 For example, you can do your laundry every Monday, **and** go to the gym on Tuesday and Thursday mornings before work or school. Always do the tasks on the same days. That way, you can plan around these important tasks **and** have time for other things. Some people don't like schedules, lists, or weekly plans. Instead, they use the notes or calendar
15 features on their cell phones. Put a reminder² for the task on your phone, **but** don't forget to do it!

These ideas can help you improve your time management.³ When you make plans and complete them, you feel good **and** can do more.

¹**"to do" list:** a list of things you need to do

²**reminder:** something that helps someone remember, like an alarm on a phone

³**time management:** being in control of your time; planning and using your time well

Things to Do!
1.
2.
3.

Monday's Tasks
9:00 a.m.
10:00 a.m.
11:00 a.m.
12:00 p.m.

2 And, But, Or

Grammar Presentation

And, *but*, and *or* are coordinating conjunctions. They connect words, phrases, and clauses.	People are busy with family and work. I like to exercise, but I don't have time for it every day. She studies in the morning or after work.

2.1 And, But, Or for Connecting Words and Phrases

Connecting Words	Time and money are valuable. She sleeps only five or six hours a night.
Connecting Phrases	I always make a schedule and look at it often. I have "to do" lists on my refrigerator but not on my phone. Do you work during the day or at night?

2.2 And, But, Or for Connecting Clauses

First Clause		Second Clause
You have more time in your day,	**and**	you feel less stressed.
Some people use their time well,	**but**	other people do not.
You can make a list,	**or**	you can schedule tasks on the same days.

2.3 Using And, But, Or

A Use *and*, *but*, and *or* to connect words, phrases, and clauses.	Time and money are valuable. He has time but not money. Do you use schedules, or do you make "to do" lists?
B Use *and* to join two or more ideas.	Maria makes time for school, family, and work. I study and work every day. I make a "to do" list, and I check the list often during the day.
C Use *but* to show contrast or surprising information.	José works hard, but he also has fun. He always makes a schedule, but he rarely follows it.

2.3 | Using *And, But, Or* (continued)

D Use *or* to show a choice of two alternatives.	You can make lists *or* schedules. I exercise *or* do laundry after I study. Is he at school *or* at work?
E Use a comma when *and, but,* and *or* connect two clauses.	My family gets together at night, *and* we talk about our day. Sonya wakes up early, *but* she is always late for work.

Grammar Application

Exercise 2.1 Choosing *And, But, Or*

A Read the sentences about two types of people. Complete the sentences with *and, but,* or *or*. Add commas where necessary.

The Organized Person

1 Every day I wake up, *and* I make a long "to do" list.

2 I usually use the "notes" feature on my phone for important tasks _____ I always do them.

3 I don't like to forget appointments _____ be late.

4 I like to be busy _____ I feel good when I get things done.

The Disorganized Person

5 Sometimes I make lists _____ I usually lose them.

6 I have a lot of appointments _____ a lot of things to do every day.

7 I try to be on time _____ I am often late for appointments.

8 I am always busy _____ I don't get things done.

B Over to You Read the sentences in A with a partner. Which statements are true for you? Tell your partner.

Exercise 2.2 Punctuating Sentences with *And, But, Or*

A Correct the sentences below about ways to add time to a busy day. Add capital letters, periods, and commas as necessary.

1 a Jane wants to read more but she doesn't have the time

   Jane wants to read more, but she doesn't have the time.

 b now she listens to audiobooks in the car and during her breaks at work

   _____

 c she listens to a book or a podcast every day and feels good about herself

   _____

2 a James is very busy and often doesn't do his homework or study

_____

b he worries about his grades and gets very upset

_____

c finally, he talks about his problem with a classmate and they decide to help each other

_____

d he and his classmate now talk on the phone every day and work on their homework together

_____

B Group Work Make a list of four study tips. Use *and*, *but*, and *or* in your sentences.

Exercise 2.3 More *And, But, Or*

Good time management includes time for fun activities. Complete the sentences with your ideas about things you do for fun. Use *and*, *but*, or *or*.

1 On the weekends, I _watch TV and garden_ _____ .

2 Once a day, I _____ .

3 In the evenings, I _____ .

4 Sometimes I _____ .

Exercise 2.4 Vocabulary Focus: Expressions with *And* and *Or*

DATA FROM THE REAL WORLD

English has many expressions using *and* and *or*. The nouns usually occur in the order they appear below.	*Do you like peanut butter and jelly?* NOT *Do you like jelly and peanut butter?*	
Common "noun *and* noun" expressions for food	cream *and* sugar salt *and* pepper bread *and* butter	peanut butter *and* jelly fish *and* chips
Common "noun *and* noun" expressions for relationships	mom *and* dad brother *and* sister husband *and* wife	Mr. *and* Mrs. father *and* son mother *and* daughter
Other common "noun *and* noun" expressions	night *and* day men *and* women name *and* address	ladies *and* gentlemen boys *and* girls
Common expressions with *or*	cash *or* credit	coffee *or* tea
Common "adjective *and* adjective" expressions	black *and* white old *and* new	nice *and* warm

A Complete the questions.

1 Do you like ___*cream*___ and sugar with your coffee?

2 Do your _____ and dad live in the United States?

3 Do you have brothers and _____ ?

4 Do you work _____ and day?

5 Do you like black and _____ movies?

6 Do you think _____ and women have really different interests?

7 Do you put salt and _____ on your food?

8 Do you usually pay with _____ or credit?

9 Do you ever eat peanut butter and _____ sandwiches?

10 Do you prefer _____ or tea?

B Pair Work Take turns asking and answering the questions in A with a partner. Use complete sentences in your answers.

A *Do you like cream and sugar with your coffee?*
B *I like sugar, but I don't like cream.*

3 *Because*

Grammar Presentation

Because introduces the reason for or cause of something.	EFFECT CAUSE *People feel stressed because there is not enough time.*

3.1 *Because* for Connecting Clauses

A *Because* shows a cause-and-effect relationship.	EFFECT CAUSE *I am always late because I don't like to get up early.*
Clauses with *because* must have a subject and a verb.	SUBJECT VERB *Some people send e-mail reminders because they want to remember their tasks.*

3.1 *Because* for Connecting Clauses *(continued)*

B A clause with *because* is <u>not</u> a complete sentence. It needs the main clause to form a complete sentence.

MAIN CLAUSE
I am always late <u>because</u> I don't like to get up early.
NOT *I am always late. ~~Because I don't like to get up early.~~*

C *Because* can come before or after the main clause. Use a comma when *because* comes first in a sentence.

MAIN CLAUSE
<u>Because</u> *I don't like to get up early, I am always late.*
MAIN CLAUSE
I am always late <u>because</u> *I don't like to get up early.*

D In speaking, you can answer a question starting with *because*. Do not do this in writing.

Why are you at school?
Say: *Because I want to learn English.*

 # Grammar Application

Exercise 3.1 Cause-and-Effect Relationships with *Because*

Match the effect on the left with the cause on the right.

1 John is tired ___c___

2 Tanya is usually late _____

3 Dan is often hungry _____

4 Eric walks slowly _____

5 Sue takes her brother to school _____

6 Maya and Sara sleep late _____

7 Jack takes classes at night _____

a because his foot hurts.

b because he never eats breakfast.

c because he doesn't sleep enough.

d because he works during the day.

e because she doesn't put reminders on her phone.

f because their mother doesn't have time.

g because they work until midnight.

Exercise 3.2 The Position of *Because*

 Put *because* in the correct place in each sentence. Add commas where necessary. Then listen and compare your answers.

Bob, Jamal, Tony, and Leo are roommates. They study at the local community college. Each roommate has a problem with time.

                  because

1 Leo works at night he goes to school during the day.

2 Tony can only study in the mornings he thinks more clearly then.

3 Bob's bus arrives after 8 o'clock he is always late.

4 Jamal can't study at home his roommates are too noisy.

5 Leo forgets to write his assignments down he often misses them.

6 Tony and Jamal sometimes miss class they play basketball instead.

Exercise 3.3 Combining Sentences with *Because*

Label each clause with *C* for "cause" and *E* for "effect." Then combine the sentences with *because*. Do not change the order of the clauses.

1 *E* Brendon does well in class.   *C* He studies every day.

   Brendon does well in class because he studies every day.

2 *C* Tanya forgets to set her alarm.   *E* She is often late for work.

   Because Tanya forgets to set her alarm, she is often late for work.

3 _____ Alan has three reminders about   _____ He doesn't want to forget about it.
the meeting on his phone.

4 _____ Wanda is always hungry at work.   _____ She doesn't have time for lunch.

5 _____ Karin starts work very early.   _____ She drinks a lot of coffee.

6 _____ Blanca works during the day.   _____ She takes night classes.

7 _____ Jared keeps a "to do" list.   _____ He has a lot of work.

Complete the sentences. Make them true for you.

1 I take English classes because _____.

2 I wake up at _____ because _____.

      (time)

3 I live in _____ because _____.

      (town/city)

4 I like _____ because _____.

      (class)

5 I go to bed at _____ because _____.

      (time)

4 Avoid Common Mistakes ⚠

1   **Do not use a comma when you join two words or two phrases.**

Lisa creates a schedule ⁄ and a list every day.

2   **Use a comma when you join two clauses with *and, but,* and *or*.**

I need to study for the test ‸ and then I have to work!

3   **Use *and* to add information. Use *but* to show a contrast. Use *or* to show a choice.**

                but
Sam is always late, ~~and~~ he gets his work done.

4   **Do not use a comma if *because* is in the second part of the sentence.**

Jake is always on time ⁄ because he takes the 8:00 bus to school every day.

   But do use a comma if *because* is in the first part of the sentence.
Because Lily makes a daily schedule ‸ she never forgets to do her tasks.

5   **Use *because* to state the reason (cause) for something. The other part of the sentence states the result (effect).**

Because Kylie writes her assignments on her calendar,
~~Kylie writes her assignments on her calendar because~~ she doesn't forget them.
Kylie doesn't forget her assignments because
~~Because Kylie doesn't forget her assignments,~~ she writes them on her calendar.

Editing Task

Read the story about Professor Kwan's class on time management. Find and correct nine more mistakes.

A Useful Class

Every year, Professor Kwan teaches a class on time management. Many students like to take her class. Sometimes the class fills up quickly/because it is so popular. Students know that they need to register early – in person and online. This is the first lesson of the time-management class.

5   In this class, Professor Kwan talks about different ways for students to organize their time. Her students often complain about the stress they have but how little time they have. Professor Kwan always tells her students to buy a calendar. She says students can use an electronic calendar but a paper calendar. Because her students get organized they use their calendar every day. She tells students to find time to

10 study at least once a day – either after school and at night. When students plan their time well, they feel in control and confident.

This is not the only thing that Professor Kwan teaches in the class. Students have a lot of stress because it is also important to find time to relax, and exercise. Professor Kwan's class is so popular, because all students need help with time management. At the

15 end of her class, students have less stress and they have great time-management skills!

5 Academic Writing

Writing Formal Emails

Brainstorm 〉 Organize 〉 Write 〉 Edit

In this unit (11), you are going to plan, write, and revise a formal email.

> Write an email to a professor.

Exercise 5.1 Preparing to Write

Work with a partner. Ask and answer the questions.

1 Do you write emails to your professors? What do you write about?

2 Look at the reasons. Put a check (√) when it is okay to email a professor.

☐ You are sick and will miss class.

☐ You don't like your project group.

☐ You want to turn your homework in late because you are tired.

☐ You need help with a lesson.

☐ You aren't ready for a test. You don't want to take it on the test day.

3 What things should you do when you write to a professor?

4 What things should you NOT do when you write to a professor?

Exercise 5.2 Comparing Emails

Read the two emails from students to their professor. Which one is better? Why?

Subject: Appointment request

Dear Professor Thompson,

I am a student in your Math 124 class. I have questions about this morning's lesson, and I need your help. I would like to talk to you this afternoon, but I can't come during office hours because I have to work at the library then. Could I make an appointment to see you at 1:30 p.m.?

Sincerely,
Magda Koch

Subject: Hi from Lily

Hi,

I'm Lily. I'm busy. Because I have a lot of homework. And I gotta take a test in another class tommorrow. I wanna turn in my project next week. Okay? Thanks.

Lily

Exercise 5.3 Comprehension Check

Work with a partner. Ask and answer the questions.
1 What does Magda want to do?
2 When does Magda want to meet? Why?
3 What does Lily want to do? Why?

Exercise 5.4 Noticing the Grammar and Structure

Look at the emails again and complete the tasks. Compare your answers with a partner's.
1 Underline *and* and *because* in each email. Which student uses these conjunctions correctly?
2 Read the chart and check (√) the correct answer.

Which student . . .	Magda	Lily
a is polite?		
b writes full names?		
c uses slang?		
d gives a good reason?		
e probably edited her email?		

Writing Emails to Professors

Students often write emails to their professors to ask for help or permission. Here are some guidelines for writing them:
• Include a clear topic in the "Subject" line.
• Do not use slang or the professor's first name.
• Write politely and clearly.
• Use complete sentences with correct grammar.
• Check your email for mistakes before you send it.

Exercise 5.5 Applying the Skill

Use the guidelines to improve Lily's email on page 144. Compare your edits with a partner's.

My Writing

Exercise 5.6 Writing a Formal Email

Follow the steps to write an email to your professor.
1 Think of a good reason to write an email to your professor.
2 Use information questions to brainstorm and organize ideas for your email.
3 Follow the guidelines to write your email.
4 Work with a partner. Give each other feedback. Then revise and edit your email.

1 Grammar in the Real World

A Do you know people who don't give up easily? Read the article. What do you learn about this band?

B Comprehension Check **Are these sentences true or false? Use the article to help you. Correct the false sentences.**

1 The executive traveled to London in December 1961.   True   False

2 The executive invited the band to London.   True   False

3 The band went to London and played on New Year's Eve.   True   False

4 The company didn't call the band immediately.   True   False

5 The band signed a contract with another company.   True   False

C Notice **Answer the questions. Use the article to help you.**

1 Can you find the past forms of these verbs in the article?

Present	travel	invite	play	wait	sign
Simple Past					

2 What do the simple past verbs in question 1 have in common?

3 Can you find the past forms of these verbs in the article?

Base Form	go	think	have	tell	become
Simple Past					

4 How are these simple past verbs different from the verbs in question 1?

A Band That Didn't Give Up¹

¹**give up:** stop trying
²**inventor:** someone who designs or create new things
³**discouraged:** not confident to try again
⁴**executive:** person in a high position in a company who manages and makes decisions
⁵**audition:** short performance given to show ability
⁶**out:** not fashionable; not popular
⁷**contract:** written legal agreement

Writers, artists, singers, and inventors² often feel discouraged³ when others tell them they are not good enough. Some people give up. Others, like a group of young musicians in the 1960s, don't let it stop them.

5   In December 1961, a record company executive⁴ **traveled** to Liverpool, England. He **went** to listen to a new rock 'n' roll band. The executive **thought** the band **had** talent and **invited** them to an audition⁵ in London. The group **went** to London and **played** on New Year's Day 1962. After the audition, they **went** home and **waited** for a phone call.
10   They **didn't hear** any news for weeks.

Finally, the company executive **told** the band manager, "Guitar groups are on the way out,⁶ Mr. Epstein." So the record company **didn't give** the band a contract.⁷

But the band **didn't give up**. In the end, they **signed** a contract with
15   another company and **became** a very famous band: The Beatles.

2 Simple Past Statements: Regular Verbs

Grammar Presentation

The simple past describes events that started and ended before now.	*In 1961, he traveled to Liverpool.* *The band played for two hours.* *They didn't hear any news for weeks.*

2.1 Affirmative Statements

Subject	Simple Past Verb	
I You We They He/She/It	**started**	in 1962.

2.2 Negative Statements

Subject	*Did + Not*	Base Form of Verb	
I You We They He/She/It	**did not** **didn't**	**sign**	a contract.

2.3 Using Simple Past Statements

A Use the simple past for events that started and ended in the past.	 the past now
It can be one event or repeated events.	*He traveled to Liverpool.* *The band played in clubs every week.* *They didn't hear any news.*
B You can use the simple past to describe a feeling in the past.	*He didn't like the band.*

2.4 Spelling: Regular Simple Past Verbs

A For most verbs, add -ed.	*work → worked*
B For verbs ending in e, add -d.	*live → lived*
C For verbs ending in consonant + y, change y to i and add -ed.	*study → studied*

2.4 Spelling: Regular Simple Past Verbs *(continued)*

D For verbs ending in vowel + *y*, add *-ed*.	*play → play**ed***
E For one-syllable verbs ending in consonant-vowel-consonant, double the consonant.	*plan → plan**ned***
F Do not double the consonant if the verb ends in *-x* or *-w*.	*show → show**ed***
G For two-syllable verbs ending in consonant-vowel-consonant and stressed on the first syllable, do not double the consonant.	*travel → trave**led***
H For two-syllable verbs ending in consonant-vowel-consonant and stressed on the second syllable, double the consonant.	*control → control**led***
🌐 Here are some of the most common regular simple past verbs.	called wanted started happened worked lived tried moved looked talked liked decided

▸ Spelling and Pronunciation Rules for Regular Verbs in Simple Past: See page A21.
▸ Common Regular and Irregular Verbs: See page A15.

🖥 Grammar Application

Exercise 2.1 Affirmative Simple Past Statements: Regular Verbs

Complete the sentences about The Beatles. Use the simple past form of the verbs in parentheses.

1 The Beatles first __*visited*__ (visit) the United States in 1964.

2 They _____ (land) in New York on February 7, 1964.

3 The door of the plane _____ (open).

4 The Beatles _____ (appear).

5 The fans _____ (cheer) and _____ (shout).

6 Some fans _____ (scream) and others _____ (cry).

7 The Beatles _____ (play) on *The Ed Sullivan Show* on TV.

8 About 74 million people _____ (watch) the show.

9 Their long hair _____ (shock) the country.

10 They _____ (change) popular music forever.

A Complete the first paragraph of this biography with negative simple past verbs. Use the full form *did not.*

This child _did not talk_ (talk) before the age
(1)
of four. He _____ (learn) to read before
(2)
the age of seven. He _____ (like) his
(3)
high school, and he _____ (pass) the
(4)
entrance exam for the Swiss Federal Polytechnic School,
a university in Zurich. One teacher _____
(5)
(believe) that he was intelligent at all. However, this boy
_____ (stop) working hard. His teachers
(6)
_____ (recognize) his genius, but he
(7)
_____ (listen) to their discouraging words.
(8)

B Complete the rest of the biography with simple past forms of the verbs in the box.

enjoy	explain	~~not perform~~	study
enter	graduate	show	work

He _did not perform_ well in school, but he _____ an interest in
(1)   (2)
science, and he _____ math. He _____ for a high school
(3)   (4)
diploma, and finally he _____ the university. He _____
(5)   (6)
four years later and then _____ on a Ph.D. He later _____
(7)   (8)
the laws of the universe. Who is he? _____ [The answer is on page 156.]

Exercise 2.3 Pronunciation Focus: Saying Simple Past Verbs

When the verb ends in /t/ or /d/, say -ed as an extra syllable /ɪd/ or /əd/.	**/ɪd/ or /əd/** /t/ wai**t** → waited /d/ deci**de** → decided
When the verb ends in /f/, /k/, /p/, /s/, /ʃ/, and /tʃ/, say -ed as /t/.	**/t/** /f/ lau**gh** → laughed /s/ mi**ss** → missed /k/ loo**k** → looked /ʃ/ fini**sh** → finished /p/ sto**p** → stopped /tʃ/ wat**ch** → watched
For verbs that end in other consonant and vowel sounds, say -ed as /d/.	**/d/** list**en** → listened play → played cha**nge** → changed ag**ree** → agreed li**ve** → lived borr**ow** → borrowed

A Listen and repeat the verbs in the chart above.

B Pair Work Add simple past endings to the verbs below. Then read the sentences aloud with a partner. Do the verbs have an extra syllable? Check (✓) *Yes* or *No*.

	Yes	No
1 A friend **call**_ed_ me last night.		✓
2 I **invite**_d_ her to dinner.	✓	
3 We **talk**_____ about music.		
4 She **want**_____ to get an old album from the 1960s for her grandfather.		
5 We **laugh**_____ about the old-fashioned records.		
6 We **look**_____ for the album on the Internet.		
7 I **download**_____ the music files.		
8 We **play**_____ them.		
9 They **sound**_____ funny.		
10 We **forward**_____ the music files to her grandfather.		
11 He **listen**_____ to the songs.		
12 Then he **delete** them. Not all music from the 1960s is good.		

C Over to You Tell a partner about four things you did last night. Use some of the verbs in this exercise.

I watched TV last night.

yesterday	last . . .	. . . ago	Prepositions
yesterday yesterday morning yesterday evening	last night last week / month / year last Friday / June / spring	two days ago six weeks ago 10 months / years ago a long time ago	in 2007 on June 19 at 7:30 before / after the audition

Time expressions usually come at the end of a sentence.	*I listened to a Beatles album last night.* *The Beatles became famous in 1962.*
Time expressions can also come at the start of a sentence when they are very important.	*After the audition, they went home and waited.* *In 1961, a record company executive traveled to Liverpool.*

Complete the sentences about a famous poet. Use the words from the box. Some words are used more than once.

after	ago	in	last	on

1 I borrowed a book of poems from the library __*last*__ week.

2 The poet lived in Massachusetts over 100 years _____.

3 She published only seven poems _____ her lifetime.

4 She died at the age of 55 _____ May 15, 1886.

5 _____ the poet's death, her sister discovered over 1,800 poems in her room.

6 Her first book of poems appeared four years after she died, _____ 1890.

7 T. H. Johnson published a complete collection of her poems _____ 1955.

8 I prepared a presentation about her for class _____ night.

1830–1886

Pair Work **When was the last time you or a friend did these things? Ask and answer questions with a partner. Write sentences about your partner.**

1 borrow a book from the library *Marie borrowed a book from the library three weeks ago.*

2 listen to a podcast _____

3 laugh or cry at a movie _____

4 move to another apartment or house _____

5 try really hard to do something _____

6 travel to another city _____

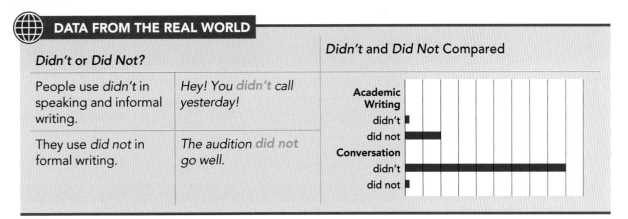

DATA FROM THE REAL WORLD

Didn't or Did Not?		Didn't and Did Not Compared
People use *didn't* in speaking and informal writing.	Hey! You *didn't* call yesterday!	
They use *did not* in formal writing.	The audition *did not* go well.	

Rewrite these sentences about the famous poet Emily Dickinson for academic writing. Change the contractions.

1 Emily Dickinson didn't publish a lot of poems in her lifetime.

 Emily Dickinson did not publish a lot of poems in her lifetime.

2 Even her family didn't know about the 1,800 poems in her room.

_____

3 In the nineteenth century, some critics didn't like her work, but she continued to write for herself.

_____

4 She didn't write like other poets.

_____

5 She didn't use correct punctuation.

_____

6 In the 1950s, poetry experts published her work again. This time, they didn't edit it.

_____

3 Simple Past Statements: Irregular Verbs

Grammar Presentation

Irregular simple past verbs don't end in -ed.	In 1961, he *went* to Liverpool. The company *made* a big mistake.

3.1 Irregular Verbs

AFFIRMATIVE STATEMENTS				NEGATIVE STATEMENTS				
Subject	Simple Past Irregular Verb			Subject	Did + Not	Base Form of Verb		
I You We They He / She / It	**became**	popular.		I You We They He / She / It	**did not didn't**	**become**	popular.	

3.2 Using Irregular Simple Past Verbs

A 🌐 Here are the most common irregular verbs.	come → came make → made do → did put → put get → got read → read go → went say → said have → had see → saw
B Be careful with the verb *do*.	I *did* my homework last night. I *didn't do* my homework this morning.

▶ Irregular Verbs: See page A16.

Grammar Application

Exercise 3.1 Simple Past Statements with Irregular Verbs

A Make guesses about things your partner did yesterday. Use the verbs in parentheses. Write affirmative and negative sentences.

1 You _____*didn't do*_____ (do) your homework last night.

2 You _____ (read) your e-mail after dinner.

3 You _____ (get up) late yesterday morning.

4 You _____ (come) to school early today.

5 You _____ (go) to work last night.

6 You _____ (make) a wonderful dinner yesterday.

7 You _____ (see) a movie in a theater last weekend.

8 You _____ (read) the news this morning.

9 You _____ (have) breakfast this morning.

10 You _____ (see) the weather report this morning.

B Pair Work Read the sentences to your partner. Are your guesses correct?

A *You didn't do your homework last night.*

B *That's true. I did my homework this morning! / That's not true. I did my homework after dinner.*

Exercise 3.2 Pronunciation Focus: Saying Irregular Simple Past Verbs

Sometimes the spelling of two verbs is the same, or similar, but the pronunciation is different.	read → read say → said BUT pay → paid hear → heard
Sometimes the letters *gh* are not pronounced.	buy → bought think → thought
When you learn an irregular verb, learn the pronunciation, too.	

A Listen and repeat the verbs in the chart above. Notice the pronunciation of the irregular past forms.

B Tell a partner about something . . .

1 you bought last week.
2 you read recently.
3 your teacher said in the last class.

4 you thought about today.
5 you paid a lot of money for years ago.
6 you heard on the news today.

Exercise 3.3 More Irregular Simple Past Verbs

A Complete the descriptions with the verbs below. Can you match the pictures to the texts?

Vincent van Gogh   J. K. Rowling   Marilyn Monroe   Abraham Lincoln

1   see   not get   come

     In 1944, Norma Jean Baker ___*came*___ to see the director of a modeling agency for a job interview. Unfortunately, Baker _____ the job. The next time the director _____ her, she had a different name and was a famous movie star. Who was she? _____

2   buy   make   pay

     This artist _____ over 800 paintings, but only one person _____ one in his lifetime. The sister of a friend _____ 400 francs (about $1,600 today) for it. Who was he? _____

3

become	go	read	lose	not have

This man _____ a lot of money as a child. He _____ to school for only 18 months, but he _____ hundreds of books. As a politician, he _____ his first election. Later, he _____ an important president in U.S. history. Who was he? _____

4

become	say	write	tell	buy

This single mother _____ her first book in a café. Twenty publishers _____ her they didn't want it. Finally, one publisher _____ "Yes." Millions of people _____ the book, and it _____ a successful movie. Who is she? _____

B Group Work **Discuss the famous people in this unit. Who is the most interesting to you? Why?**

Answer to Exercise 2.2B, p. 150: Albert Einstein

4 Avoid Common Mistakes ⚠

1 **Use simple past verbs to write or talk about the past.**

started
He ~~starts~~ his career in 2002.

ate
I ~~eat~~ at a restaurant last night.

2 **After *did not / didn't*, use the base form of the verb. Do <u>not</u> use the past form.**

earn
They didn't ~~earned~~ a lot of money.

3 **For the negative, write *did not* as two words.**

did not
She ~~didnot~~ get the job.

4 **Use the correct spelling for simple past verbs.**

bought	*took*	*read*	*studied*	*dropped*	*paid*
~~buyed~~	~~taked~~	~~red~~	~~studyed~~	~~droped~~	~~payed~~

5 **The simple past negative of *have* is *did not / didn't have*. The simple past negative of *do* is *did not / didn't do*.**

didn't have
He ~~had not~~ a successful career.

did not do
She ~~did not~~ her homework last night.

Editing Task

Find and correct 10 more mistakes in this paragraph about the inventor of the lightbulb.

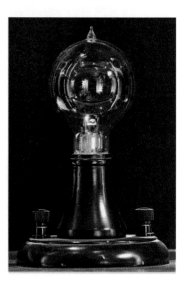

Thomas Edison was born in 1847 in Milan, Ohio. He ~~had not~~ *did not have* very much education in school. His mother taught him reading, writing, and math. Like many children at the time, he dropped out of school and got a job. At age 13, he sells newspapers and candy
5   at a railroad station. Thomas continue to learn about science by reading. At age 16, he become a telegraph operator.[1] Later, he start to invent things. In 1869, he moved to New York City. One of his inventions earned him $40,000, so he opened his first research laboratory[2] in New Jersey. He tried hundreds of times to make the
10   first lightbulb, but he had not success. However, Thomas Edison didnot give up. He learn from his mistakes. In 1879, he introduce his greatest invention, the electric light for the home. He told a reporter, "I didn't failed 1,000 times. The lightbulb was an invention with 1,000 steps."

[1]**telegraph operator:** a person who worked with a communication device that sent and received signals
[2]**research laboratory:** a building with equipment for doing scientific tests

5 Academic Writing

Narrative Paragraph

Brainstorm > Organize > Write > Edit

In this writing cycle (Units 12-15), you are going to answer the prompt below. In this unit (12), you will read about a business and then use a timeline to brainstorm ideas for your writing.

> *Write a paragraph about the history of a business.*

Exercise 5.1 Preparing to Write

Work with a partner. Ask and answer the questions.

1 What are some successful businesses you know?

2 Think of a business or company that failed. Why did it fail?

3 How does the Internet help businesses? How can it hurt businesses?

Exercise 5.2 Focusing on Vocabulary

Read the sentences. Match the words in bold to the definitions.

1 I want to own my own business. I can reach my **goal** by studying hard.

2 The Acme company **introduced** a new tablet, and it sold out in one day.

3 I shared an **office** with a coworker. It was small, and there was not a lot of space to work.

4 Many businesses have **partners**. Partners work together for success.

5 Last year I **set up** my new business in my garage, but now I have office space in a building.

a _____ (phr v) to create or establish (something) for a particular purpose

b _____ (n) a place in a building where people work

c _____ (n) someone who runs or owns a business with another person

d _____ (n) something you want to do successfully in the future

e _____ (v) to make something available to buy or use for the first time

The Story of **Google**

Google is a huge technology company. It specializes in online advertising and other Internet-related products. Larry Page and Sergey Brin started Google. They met at Stanford University in 1995. Their **goal** was to organize all of the information on the Web. Today, their company employs more than 40,000 people
5 around the world. The two **partners** created a company to make searching the Internet easy.

Google grew very quickly. Page and Brin registered the domain name Google.com in 1997. In 1998, they **set up** a small **office** in a garage and hired their first employee, Craig Silverstein. They ran their business in the garage until
10 they could move to a larger space. In 2000, people could do Internet searches in 15 languages, including Dutch, Chinese, and Korean. Today, people can search in about 150 languages. Google **introduced** a map service in 2005 called Google Maps™. The same year, it came out with a program called Google Earth™. This program allowed users to see close-up pictures of cities and neighborhoods
15 when they typed in an address. In 2006, the name "Google" became a verb in English dictionaries. This shows the company's influence on modern life.

Today, Google is a creative workplace where employees share ideas with each other. Page and Brin are available during the week to talk with their employees and answer questions. This open environment has resulted in many new ideas.
20 The company extends its services to the community, too. In 2008, it started a yearly art contest for students. Every year, the winner's artwork appears on its homepage for one day. Google believes that creativity is important, both in the workplace and in the community.

Exercise 5.3 Comprehension Check

Read the text on page 159. Write *T* (true) or *F* (false) next to the statements. Correct the false statements.

_____ **1** Google's first office was in a garage.

_____ **2** Google's only focus is on making their search engine smart and fast.

_____ **3** Google Earth teaches people how to use maps.

_____ **4** In 2006, "Google" was added to dictionaries as a verb.

Exercise 5.4 Noticing the Grammar and Structure

Work with a partner. Complete the tasks.
1 Underline the verbs in the simple past. Why are the other verbs in the simple present?
2 Which words and phrases help you understand the correct order of events? Circle them.

Exercise 5.5 Identifying Events

1 Which years in the text were important for Google? Choose 2–3 important events to discuss.

2 Work with a partner. Explain what happened and why you chose those events.

Using a Timeline to Put Past Events in Order

When writers discuss things that happened in the past, they usually put them in **chronological order**. That means they start with the event that happened first and end with the event that happened last. **Timelines** are a useful way to organize past events in chronological order.

Exercise 5.6 Applying the Skill

Place the events in Google's history at the top of the next page in the correct place on the timeline below. Write the dates above the timeline and the events below it.

a launched Google Earth & Google Maps
b employed its first worker, Craig Silverstein
c registered domain name Google.com
d Page & Brin met at Stanford
e started a student art contest
f Dictionaries added "Google" as a verb
g became possible to use Google search in 15 languages

My Writing

Exercise 5.7 Brainstorming

Choose a business you are interested in. Go online and research information about the story of the business. Use the questions to help you research.

- When did the business start?
- Who started the business?
- What challenges did the business face?
- What helped the business grow?
- How successful is the business today?

Exercise 5.8 Creating a Timeline

Write key dates and events about the business you researched on the timeline below.

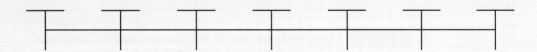

Exercise 5.9 Writing Sentences

Write a sentence about each of the main events in Exercise 5.8. Use the simple past.

_____

_____

_____

_____

_____

_____

1 Grammar in the Real World

A Do you know a business owner? Read the conversation between two students. What is unusual about Blake Mycoskie's business?

B Comprehension Check **Answer the questions.**

1 Did Blake Mycoskie win *The Amazing Race* on TV?

_____

2 When did he start TOMS Shoes?

_____

3 How many pairs of shoes did he distribute by the end of September 2010?

_____

4 What are two problems for children without shoes?

_____

C Notice **Find the questions in the conversation. Complete the questions.**

1 Did you _____ your report for class tomorrow?

2 What did he _____ ?

3 Did you _____ "shoes"?

4 Why did he _____ to sell shoes?

What form of the verb did you use to complete the questions?

A WORLD OF SHOES

Greg Hey, Liliana. **Did you finish** your report for class tomorrow?

Liliana No, but I found a really interesting businessman, Blake Mycoskie. Do you
5 remember him from that reality TV show, *The Amazing Race*?

Greg No, not really. **Did he win?**

Liliana No, he didn't, but that's not important. My report is on his *business*. It's really unusual.

10 **Greg** Why? **What did he do?** Let me guess . . . He started a cool company, and he made millions from his idea.

Liliana He started a cool company, and it helps fight poverty. He sells shoes, and . . .

15 **Greg** **Did you say** "shoes"?

Liliana Yes, he started TOMS Shoes in 2006. For every pair of shoes he sells, he donates a pair to a child in need.[1] By the end of September 2010, he distributed[2] his one
20 millionth pair.

Greg Hmm. Interesting. But **why did he decide to sell shoes?**

Liliana During *The Amazing Race*, he traveled with his sister all over the world. He saw
25 a lot of very poor people and a lot of children without shoes. A lot of these children had diseases because they walked barefoot.[3] The schools did not allow children to attend without shoes.
30 So he came up with this concept[4] of selling and donating shoes. In the future, he plans to expand[5] his business and make other products, too.

Greg Oh, I see. He's a social entrepreneur.
35 He wants to make money, but he also wants to help people.

---

[1]**in need:** not having enough money
[2]**distribute:** give something to many people
[3]**barefoot:** not wearing any shoes or socks
[4]**concept:** idea
[5]**expand:** make something bigger

2 Simple Past *Yes/No* Questions

Grammar Presentation

Simple past *Yes/No* questions ask about actions and events that happened before now.	*Did* you **finish** your report? *Did* he **do** something fun?

2.1 *Yes/No* Questions

Did	Subject	Base Form of Verb	
Did	I you we they he / she / it	**finish**	the report?

2.2 Short Answers

AFFIRMATIVE		
Yes	Subject	*Did*
Yes,	I you we they he / she / it	**did.**

NEGATIVE		
No	Subject	*Did + Not*
No,	I you we they he / she / it	**did not.** **didn't.**

2.3 Using Simple Past *Yes/No* Questions

A Questions in the simple past often use definite past-time expressions.	*Did Blake go to college in the 1990s?* *Did he start his company 11 years ago?*
B Use the contraction *didn't* in negative short answers. The full form *did not* is very formal.	*"Did Blake win The Amazing Race?"* *"No, he didn't."*
C Use pronouns in short answers.	*"Did Blake start a shoe company?"* *"Yes, he did."*
To give extra information, you can also answer *Yes/No* questions with long answers.	*"Yes, he started TOMS shoes in 2006."*

Grammar Application

Liliana heard about Blake Mycoskie and then went to a trade show[1] for entrepreneurs. Complete the questions in the simple past. Use the words in parentheses.

Liliana   _Did you have_ (you/have) a good
(1)
weekend?

Simon   Yeah, pretty good. How about you?

Liliana   Yes, very good.

Simon   _____ (you/go out)?
(2)

Liliana   Yeah. I went out with Aisha on Saturday.

Simon   Oh, _____ (you/go) somewhere
(3)
interesting?

Liliana   Yeah. We went to a trade show. There were lots of exhibits[2] from new companies.

Simon   A trade show? I didn't know you were interested in business!

Liliana   Yes, I'm very interested in it. _____ (I/tell) you about my
(4)
grandmother's company?

Simon   No.

Liliana   My grandmother had her own clothing design company, so I want to do something like that.

Simon   Really? _____ (you/see) any design companies there?
(5)

Liliana   Yeah. We saw some. A lot of the companies' owners are young entrepreneurs.

Simon   _____ (you/speak) with any interesting people?
(6)

Liliana   Yeah. I spoke with the owner of a men's tie company. He designs his own fabric.[3]

Simon   Hmm. _____ (he/have) any good ideas for you?
(7)

Liliana   Yes. He told me one thing: find a good business partner. What do you say? Do you want to be my business partner?

[1]**trade show:** a large event at which companies show and sell their products and try to increase their business
[2]**exhibit:** a collection of things people can see in public
[3]**fabric:** cloth or material

A Read Liliana's notes for her report on Blake Mycoskie. Then write the questions.

Questions About Blake Mycoskie

1 Second in "The Amazing Race"?

2 Other businesses before TOMS?

3 Sister – start the business with him?

4 Any experience in fashion?

5 Company – difficulties at the beginning?

1 he/finish _Did he finish second in "The Amazing Race"?_

2 he/have _____

3 his sister/start _____

4 he/have _____

5 the company/have _____

B Read some more information about Blake. Then answer the questions in A. First, write one short answer, and then write one long answer with extra information for each question.

When Blake Mycoskie competed in *The Amazing Race* with his sister Paige, they finished third. They lost the race by only four minutes. His sister helped him with the concept of TOMS Shoes, but he started the business by himself. He had previous experience in business, but he didn't have any experience in fashion. But he liked to design things. Before TOMS shoes, he started five other businesses, including a college laundry business and a reality TV channel. When he started TOMS, he had a lot of problems with the shoe factory.[1] Now the factory runs well, and a lot of people work for him.

[1]**factory:** a building where people use machines to produce things

1 a _No, he didn't._

   b _No, he finished third._

2 a _____

   b _____

3 a _____

   b _____

4 a _____

   b _____

5 a _____

   b _____

C Pair Work Ask and answer the questions about Blake with a partner.

A Over to You Write questions to ask a partner about last weekend. For question 5, use your own verb.

1 (do) *Did you do anything interesting?*
2 (work) _____
3 (have) _____
4 (go out) _____
5 _____

B Pair Work Ask and answer the questions with your partner. Give your partner additional information.

A *Did you do anything interesting?*   **A** *Did you go out on Saturday?*
B *No, not really. I stayed home.*   **B** *Yes, I went to . . . /No, I worked all day.*

3 Simple Past Information Questions

Grammar Presentation

Simple past information questions ask about people, things, times, and places that happened before now.	*What did he do?* *Why did he decide to make shoes?*

3.1 Information Questions

Wh- Word	Did	Subject	Base Form of Verb	
Who			write	about?
What		I	do	yesterday?
When		you	finish	our report?
What time	did	we they	begin	writing?
Where		he	visit	on vacation?
Why		she	start	a company?
How		it	save	enough money?

3.2 Using Simple Past Information Questions

A Use simple past information questions to ask for specific information about something that happened in the past.	*"Where did she study business?"* "She studied at Florida State." *"When did she graduate?"* "She graduated in 2012."
B Use *Wh-* words with *did* to ask about habits and regular activities.	*"What did she do every summer?"* "She worked at a restaurant."

3.3 Using *Wh-* Words in Simple Past Information Questions

A Use *Who* to ask about people.	*Who* did you start your company with?	My sister.
B Use *What* to ask about things.	*What* did you make?	Shoes.
C Use *When* to ask about time (days, months, years, seasons, parts of the day).	*When* did you have this idea?	Last week.
D Use *What time* to ask about clock time.	*What time* did you start work today?	At seven o'clock.
E Use *Where* to ask about places.	*Where* did you go to business school?	In Boston.
F Use *Why* to ask about reasons.	*Why* did you open a restaurant?	Because I love food.
G Use *How* to ask about manner.	*How* did you save enough money?	I saved some every month.

⌨ Grammar Application

Exercise 3.1 Simple Past Information Questions and Answers

A Shelly Hwang, an entrepreneur, started a chain of frozen yogurt stores called Pinkberry. Unscramble the words to make questions about her.

1 Why / she / to / move / did / the United States?

   Why did she move to the United States?

2 What / after / she / did / college? / do

   _____

Shelly Hwang, founder of Pinkberry

3 Who / she / with? / develop / the concept / did

_____

4 When / open / store? / she / did / her first

_____

5 What / have? / the store / did / flavors

_____

B Listen to an instructor talk about Hwang. Then write short answers to the questions in A.

1 *To study business.*
_____

2 _____

3 _____

4 _____

5 _____

4 Avoid Common Mistakes ⚠

1 Use *did* + subject + base form of the verb.

did   graduate
When you graduate̶d̶ from business school?

2 In information questions, use *did* and the base form of the main verb. Do <u>not</u> use the past form.

open   become
Where did you open̶e̶d̶ the first store? Did it becam̶e̶ a success?

3 When *do* is the main verb, use *did* + subject + *do* (base form of verb).

do
What did you at the company?

Editing Task

Find and correct the mistakes in these questions about your work experience.

work
1 Did you work̶e̶d̶ for a relative?

2 Who you worked for?

3 What did you?

4 How many hours did you worked each week?

5 How much money did you earned each week?

6 You enjoyed your job?

7 What you learned from this job?

8 Why did you stopped working?

5 Academic Writing

Narrative Paragraph

| Brainstorm | > | Organize | > | Write | > | Edit |

In Unit 12, you read about a business and used a timeline to brainstorm ideas for the prompt below. In this unit (13), you will add details to main events and use a table to plan your paragraph.

Write a paragraph about the history of a business.

Adding Details to Main Events

In a narrative paragraph, adding details to the main events makes the writing more interesting and informative. Giving examples and reasons, explaining ideas, and using adjectives are ways to add details.

These details give your readers a picture of the events in their minds. Ask yourself these questions to help add details to narrative writing:

- Who is the paragraph about?
- Why did the events happen?
- How can I give the reader a mental picture of what I am describing?
- Can I make any information more specific with dates, reasons, adjectives, or examples?
- Do the details in my narrative tell the story?

Exercise 5.1 Applying the Skill

Read a paragraph about the history of YouTube™. The sentences after the paragraph (a-d) add more details. Write the letters of the sentences in the correct places in the paragraph.

> In 2005, three friends, Chad Hurley, Steve Chen, and Jawed Karim, had an idea for an Internet business. (1)_____ They created YouTube™. Today, YouTube is the second largest search engine on the Internet, and has over a billion users. YouTube's first office was located in a simple room. (2)_____ Their first video was posted in April 2005. It was called "Me at the Zoo." (3)_____ Within five months, over a million people saw the video. Businesses began to notice YouTube and wanted to advertise on the website. In July 2006, 65,000 new videos were posted every day. In November 2006, Google bought YouTube. (4)_____

a They wanted to help people share videos on the Internet.
b It showed Karim at the zoo talking about elephants.
c They paid the incredible price of $1.65 billion.
d The room was located above a pizza restaurant in Menlo Park, California.

My Writing

Exercise 5.2 Using a Paragraph Planner

Review your timeline on page 161. Choose four important events in the history of the company, and write them in chronological order in the paragraph planner below. Add at least one detail for each event.

Main event 1	
Details	
Main event 2	
Details	
Main event 3	
Details	
Main event 4	
Details	

Exercise 5.3 Adding More Details

Work with a partner. Complete the tasks.

1 Ask your partner simple past *Wh-* questions about the events in their planner in Exercise 5.2 to help brainstorm more details.
2 Use the answers to add interesting details, such as dates, adjectives, reasons, and examples, to your planner.

Simple Past of *Be*

1 Grammar in the Real World

A What were you like as a child? Read the magazine article about
Sheryl Sandberg. What was she like as a child?

B Comprehension Check Do these words describe Sheryl
Sandberg as a child or as an adult? Check (✓) the correct answers.
Some words describe both. Use the article to help you.

	As a Child	As an Adult
1 very famous	☐	☐
2 successful	☐	☐
3 busy	☐	☐
4 interested in friends	☐	☐

C Notice Read the sentences. Circle *was* or *were*. Use the article to
help you.

1 Her father **was / were** an eye doctor.

2 Her mother **was / were** a teacher.

3 Her parents **was / were** busy.

4 Sheryl **was / were** a good student.

5 She **was / were** always busy.

6 People **was / were** interested in
the Internet.

When do you use *was*? When do you use *were*?

Sheryl Sandberg:
A BUSINESS SUCCESS STORY

Sheryl Sandberg is a very famous business person. She worked at Google and **was** the first woman to be a director at Facebook. She wrote two very popular books. Today she is a billionaire. However, Sheryl Sandberg started her life in an
5 ordinary family. She **was** born in Washington, D.C. in 1969. Her family moved to Miami, Florida, when she **was** two years old. Her mother **was** an English teacher, and her father **was** an eye doctor. Her parents **were** very busy with their jobs, Sheryl, and her brother and sister.

10 Sheryl **was** a very good student at North Miami Beach High School. She studied a lot and taught exercise classes after school. She had a group of very close friends. Her friends say she **was not** interested in television or movies. She **was** always busy doing things.

15 In 1987, Sheryl went to Harvard University and then worked in Washington, D.C. She moved to California and **was** very successful at Google. People **were** interested in using the Internet to make new friends and write to old friends, so Sheryl got a job at Facebook. She made the company bigger and
20 helped it make more money. Sheryl learned a lot at Google and Facebook, and she wrote a book to help other women who want to be successful in business. More than 2.25 million people bought Sheryl's book.

2 Simple Past of *Be*: Affirmative and Negative Statements

Grammar Presentation

The simple past of *be* describes people, places, or things in the past.	*Her home was in Florida.* *Her parents were busy.*

2.1 Statements

AFFIRMATIVE

Subject	Was / Were	
I He She It	**was**	in the computer lab.
We You They	**were**	

NEGATIVE

Subject	Was / Were + Not	
I He She It	**was not** **wasn't**	in class.
We You They	**were not** **weren't**	

2.2 Using Simple Past of *Be*

A Use the simple past of *be* to talk or write about people, places, or things in the past. *Be* has two past forms: *was* and *were*.	*She was a director.* *The students were in their class.* *I was not in the computer lab.* *They were not bored.*
B Use *was/were + born* to say when or where someone was born.	*She was born in Washington, D.C. in 1969.*
C *Not* comes after *be* in negative statements.	*She was not interested in television.*
D In speaking, you can use the contractions *wasn't* and *weren't* in negative statements.	*Sheryl wasn't interested in television.* *They weren't happy.*
E We often use past time expressions with the simple past of *be*: *ten years ago/yesterday/this morning/last week/ in the past*	*In 1987, Sheryl was a student.* *We were in California last week.*
Past time expressions can go either at the beginning of a sentence or at the end of a sentence.	

Grammar Application

Exercise 2.1 Simple Past of *Be*: Affirmative and Negative Statements

A Read the descriptions of three famous women. Complete the sentences with *was/wasn't* or *were/weren't*. Write the names on the lines.

| Oprah Winfrey | Taylor Swift | Penélope Cruz |

1 _____

She _____was_____ born in Madrid, Spain, in 1974.
(1)
Her father _____ an auto mechanic[1] and her mother
(2)
_____ a hairdresser.[2] She studied ballet and jazz dance
(3)
as a child. When she _____ a teenager, she started
(4)
acting. At 17, she _____ in her first film.
(5)

[1]**auto mechanic:** someone who repairs cars
[2]**hairdresser:** a person who cuts and styles hair (usually women's hair)

2 _____

She _____ born in Mississippi in 1954. Her mother
(6)
and father _____ very poor. Her father _____ a
(7)   (8)
barber.[3] When she _____ in high school, she got her
(9)
first radio job. She _____ a student at Tennessee State
(10)
University for several years. She got her first TV job in 1972.
By age 32, she _____ a millionaire.
(11)

[3]**barber:** a person who cuts men's hair

3 _____

She _____ born in Pennsylvania in 1989.
(12)
As a child, she loved to write and wrote in her diary every
day. When she _____ in the fourth grade, she won a
(13)
poetry contest.[4] She began to write songs, and she sang
at festivals and contests. She _____ (not) shy, and she
(14)
liked to perform. In high school, she _____ (not) very
(15)
popular. Other students _____ (not) friendly with her.
(16)
Now she's very popular.

[4]**contest:** a competition to win a prize

B Complete the sentences with *was* and *wasn't*. Use the information in A to help you.

1 Penélope Cruz __wasn't__ born in the United States.

2 As a child, Taylor Swift _____ a songwriter.

3 Oprah Winfrey's family _____ wealthy.

4 As a child, Penélope Cruz _____ a dancer.

5 By age 32, Oprah Winfrey _____ poor.

6 Oprah Winfrey's father _____ a TV star.

7 Penélope Cruz _____ a teenager when she started acting.

Exercise 2.2 Simple Past of *Be*: More Affirmative and Negative Statements

A Over to You **What were you like as a child? Write six sentences about you and your family members. Write three sentences with *was/were* and three sentences with *wasn't/weren't*. Use the words in the box and your own ideas.**

a bad student	active	busy	funny	intelligent	short	talkative
a good student	bored	friendly	happy	quiet	shy	tall

I was very shy. I wasn't a good student. My father was a mechanic.

was/were

1 _____

2 _____

3 _____

wasn't/weren't

1 _____

2 _____

3 _____

B Pair Work **Tell your partner what you were like as a child and about your family members.**

A *I was very shy. I wasn't very talkative.*

B *Really? That's surprising. What about your brothers and sisters?*

A *They weren't shy at all.*

3 Simple Past of *Be*: Questions and Answers

Grammar Presentation

Yes/No questions and information questions with the simple past of *be* ask about people, places, and things in the past.	"**Were** you in college last year?" "No, I **wasn't**." "When **were** you in college?" "I **was** in college three years ago."

3.1 Yes/No Questions

Was / Were	Subject	
Was	I he she it	very smart?
Were	we you they	in college?

3.2 Short Answers

AFFIRMATIVE

Yes	Subject	Was / Were
Yes,	I he she it	**was.**
	we you they	**were.**

NEGATIVE

No	Subject	Was / Were + Not
No,	I he she it	**was not.** **wasn't.**
	we you they	**were not.** **weren't.**

3.3 Using Yes/No Questions with Simple Past of *Be*

A We often use past time expressions in *Yes/No* questions with the simple past of *be*: *ten years ago/yesterday/this morning/last week*

Past time expressions go at the end of a question.

Were you in college last year?
Was Bill famous in 1955?
Was she born in 2003?

B Use the contractions *wasn't/weren't* in negative short answers.

"Was she a dancer?"   *"No, she wasn't."*
"Were they wealthy?"   *"No, they weren't."*

C You can also answer with additional information.

"Was she a dancer?"   *"No, she was a songwriter."*
"Were they wealthy?"   *"No, they were very poor."*

3.4 Information Questions

Wh- Word	Was / Were	Subject	
Who		your best friend	as a child?
What	**was**	your favorite class	last semester?
When		her birthday party?	
What time		the meeting	on Monday?
Where		his partners?	
Why	**were**	they	successful?
How		the concerts	the other night?
How old		their children	in 2017?

3.5 Using *Wh-* Words with Simple Past of *Be*

A Use *Who* to ask about people.	*Who* was the first female director at Facebook?	Sheryl Sandberg.
B Use *What* to ask about things.	*What* was your favorite class last semester?	English.
C Use *When* to ask about time (days, months, years, seasons, parts of the day).	*When* was your sister born?	In April.
D Use *What time* to ask about clock time.	*What time* was your class?	At eight o'clock.
E Use *Where* to ask about places.	*Where* were you born?	In Tokyo.
F Use *Why* to ask about reasons.	*Why* were they excited?	Because they won the game.
G Use *How* to ask what something was like.	*How* was the play?	It was great.
H Use *How old* to ask about age.	*How old* was your brother last year?	He was 18.

⌨ Grammar Application

Exercise 3.1 Simple Past of *Be: Yes/No* Questions

A Tanya's class assignment is to interview her grandfather. Complete her questions with *Was* or *Were*.

1 _____*Were*_____ you born in New York City?

2 _____ your family large?

3 _____ your brother a good student?

4 _____ you and your brother good friends?

5 _____ your sisters nice to you?

6 _____ you and your sisters the same age?

7 _____ your father's store near the house?

B Pair Work Listen to the conversation between Tanya and her grandfather. Write short answers about the grandfather's life to the questions in A. Then compare your answers with a partner.

1   *No, he wasn't.*

2

3

4

5

6

7

Exercise 3.2 Simple Past of *Be*: *Yes/No* Questions and Information Questions

A Read the paragraph about a childhood photograph. Then write information questions and answers about the photograph.

My great-grandmother was born in 1901 in Wisconsin. She was born at 12:10 in the morning. She was the first of two children. Her father was a store owner, and her mother was a teacher. They lived in a small town. I once saw a photograph of her
5   house. The house had two floors, and it was very simple. There was no paint on the house, but it was well built. There was a nice front porch with several chairs and some flowers. My great-grandmother and her father were in the photo. Her father was happy, but she was angry because she hated sitting for pictures. She was about
10   three years old in the photo. She was upset but very cute.

1 (When / she born)   *When was she born?*   *She was born in 1901.*

2 (Where / she born)

3 (What time / she born)

4 (What / her father's job)

5 (What / her mother's job)

6 (Who / in the photo)

7 (What / on the porch)

8 (Why / she angry)

9 (How old / she in the photo)

B Over to You Write questions to ask a partner about his or her childhood. Write *Yes/No* questions and information questions. Use *was/were* and the words in the box or your own ideas.

born	favorite family activity	school
brothers	favorite games	sisters
chores[1]	favorite room in your house	your bedroom
father's/mother's job	favorite toys	

Where were you born?

1 _____
2 _____
3 _____
4 _____
5 _____
6 _____
7 _____
8 _____

[1]**chore:** a job that is often boring but that is important, like washing the dishes

C Pair Work Ask and answer the questions about childhood from B. Take turns.

A *Were you born in the United States?*
B *No, I was born in Thailand.*

4 Avoid Common Mistakes ⚠

1 With *I / he / she / it* or a singular noun, use *was*.

    was
He ~~were~~ a famous artist.

2 With *you / we / they* or a plural noun, use *were*.

    were
My brothers ~~was~~ usually nice to me.

3 Use the correct form with *born*.

    were you born   was born
When ~~was you born~~?   I ~~born~~ in 1980.

Editing Task

Find and correct seven more mistakes in the questions and answers about Yo-Yo Ma.

          was
A When ~~were~~ Yo-Yo Ma born?

B He born in 1955.

A He born in the United States?

B No, he wasn't. He was born in France.

5 **A** Were his parents French?

B No, they was not. They was Chinese.

A Were his parents musicians?

B Yes, they was talented musicians.

A How old was he when he first played the cello?

10 **B** He was four.

A How old were he when he moved to New York City?

B He were five.

A How many albums does he have?

B Currently, he has more than 75 albums.

Yo-Yo Ma, cellist

5 Academic Writing

Narrative Paragraph

Brainstorm > Organize > **Write** > Edit

In Unit 13, you learned how to add details to main events and used a paragraph planner for the prompt below. In this unit (14), you will use time-order transition signals and then write the first draft of your paragraph.

> *Write a paragraph about the history of a business.*

Exercise 5.1 Noticing the Structure

Read the narrative paragraph. Work with a partner. Ask and answer the questions.

> Google is a big, successful company now, but when it started, it was very small. In 1995, Larry Page and Sergey Brin were students at Stanford University. They met when Larry was 22 and Sergey was 21, and they became good friends. Two years later, they registered the domain name Google.com. Soon after that, they turned a small garage into an office, and they hired their very first employee. Page and Brin did not stay in the garage for long. The company grew very quickly and moved several times. Finally, in 2003, Google set up its company headquarters in Mountain View, California. Gmail came out a year later, and it was a big success. Next, Google Maps™ and Google Earth™ were launched. In 2005, Google was worth more than $52 billion dollars. Today, it is one of the richest companies in the world.

1 What is the topic sentence?
2 How did the writer organize the events and ideas in the paragraph?
3 Which details make the information more interesting for the reader?

Using Time-Order Transition Signals

Writers use **time-order transition signals** when they write narrative paragraphs. Time-order transition signals help readers better understand when the main events in a story took place.

Look at the words in bold in the paragraph below. Notice how the writer used different signals to order the main events in the story of YouTube™.

> Three friends started an Internet video business called YouTube™ **in 2005. A year later**, YouTube was one of the fastest-growing websites on the Internet. It had more than 65,000 new videos on its site. **Soon after that**, Google bought YouTube for over one billion dollars.

Note: Use a comma (,) after transition signals that come at the beginning of a sentence.

Exercise 5.2 Understanding the Skill

Read the narrative paragraph about Google in Exercise 5.1.
Find and underline the time-order transition signals.
Compare your answers with a partner's.

My Writing

Exercise 5.3 Applying the Skill

Look at the main events in your paragraph planner on page 171. Write a sentence for each of the main events. Use a time-order transition signal and the simple past.

1 _____

2 _____

3 _____

4 _____

Exercise 5.4 Writing Your Paragraph

Follow the steps below to write a narrative paragraph.

1 Review your paragraph planner and add any new information.

2 Write a topic sentence that includes the topic and main idea of your paragraph.

_____

_____

3 Write the first draft of your paragraph. Use the correct simple past forms.

_____

_____

_____

_____

_____

_____

_____

Past Time Clauses with *When, Before,* and *After*

Luck and Loss

1 Grammar in the Real World

A Do you ever get e-mails with the message "You won a contest" or "We need to check your bank account"? Read the web article. Why was Sandra Walters lucky?

B Comprehension Check **Circle the correct answers.**

1 Where did Sandra receive the e-mail?

   a at home   **b** at work   **c** at the bank

2 How much money did the man ask her to send to a bank outside the United States?

   a $1,000   **b** $2.5 million   **c** $25

3 Why did Sandra give her credit card number to the man?

   a because she didn't have a bank   **b** because it was quick   **c** to pay the fee

4 When did she realize it was a scam?

   a when she got home   **b** after she finished the call   **c** when she called her credit card company

C Notice **What did Sandra do first? For each pair of sentences, write *1* and *2*. Use the article to help you.**

1 _____ Sandra was surprised.   _____ Sandra read her e-mail.

2 _____ She called the number.   _____ She went home.

3 _____ She said she didn't have $1,000.   _____ The man asked for her credit card number.

4 _____ She began to think.   _____ She put the phone down.

5 _____ She realized her mistake.   _____ She called her credit card company.

INTERNET LOTTERY
SCAM[1]

When Sandra Walters opened her e-mail one day at work last year, she was surprised. One message said, "Congratulations. You are the lucky winner of $2.5 million in the National Millionaire's Contest. Call this number." **When Sandra got home**, she called the number and spoke
5 to a man who seemed very nice. The man told her to send a $1,000 fee[2] to a bank outside the United States. **When Sandra said she didn't have $1,000**, the man said, "No problem. I can charge your credit card." She gave him her credit card number, her bank account number, and her address. The man promised to send her a check for $2.5 million the next
10 day. Then he hung up. **After Sandra put the phone down**, she began to think. What was this contest? She didn't remember entering any contest. How did she win?

Unfortunately, it's a common story. There is no National Millionaire's Contest. In a real contest, you never pay a fee **before you receive your**
15 **prize**. Sandra wasn't a winner. She was the victim[3] of a scam . . . almost. Luckily, Sandra realized her mistake and called her credit card company. They canceled[4] the card **before the criminals[5] used it**.

Don't fall for[6] this scam. An e-mail message that asks for personal information is probably a scam. Just delete it!

[1]**scam:** a dishonest way of making money
[2]**fee:** money you pay for a service
[3]**victim:** someone who suffers from violence, illness, or bad luck
[4]**cancel:** stop something from working
[5]**criminal:** a person who has done something illegal
[6]**fall for:** believe something is true when it's not

2 Past Time Clauses with *When*, *Before*, and *After*

Grammar Presentation

<table>
<tr>
<td>Time clauses show the order of events in the past. They can begin with *when*, *before*, and *after*.</td>
<td>

FIRST EVENT   SECOND EVENT

After Sandra put the phone down, *she began to think.*

</td>
</tr>
</table>

2.1 Time Clauses

Time Clause		Main Clause
When **Before** **After**	**I get to work,**	I check my e-mail.

Main Clause	Time Clause	
I check my e-mail	**when** **before** **after**	**I get to work.**

2.2 Main Clauses and Time Clauses

<table>
<tr>
<td>

A A clause has a subject and a verb.

</td>
<td>

SUBJECT VERB
  She was surprised.

      SUBJECT   VERB
When **Sandra opened** her e-mail, . . .

</td>
</tr>
<tr>
<td>

B A main clause is a complete sentence. It has a subject and a verb.

</td>
<td>

SUBJECT   VERB
Sandra called the number.

SUBJECT VERB
  She began to think.

</td>
</tr>
<tr>
<td>

C A time clause can begin with *when*, *before*, or *after*. It has a subject and a verb. However, it is <u>not</u> a complete sentence. A time clause always goes with a main clause.

</td>
<td>

  SUBJECT VERB   SUBJECT VERB
When **she got** home, she called the number.

    SUBJECT   VERB   SUBJECT VERB
After **Sandra put** the phone down, she began to think.

</td>
</tr>
<tr>
<td>

D You can add a time clause to a main clause to say when something happened.

</td>
<td>

    MAIN CLAUSE   TIME CLAUSE
Sandra called the number **when she got home.**

      TIME CLAUSE   MAIN CLAUSE
After Sandra put the phone down, *she began to think.*

</td>
</tr>
</table>

2.2 Main Clauses and Time Clauses *(continued)*

E A time clause can go before or after the main clause.

When the time clause comes first, use a comma after it.

> TIME CLAUSE   MAIN CLAUSE
> *When Sandra opened her e-mail,* she was surprised.
>
> TIME CLAUSE   MAIN CLAUSE
> *After Sandra put the phone down,* she began to think.

When the time clause comes second, do not use a comma.

> MAIN CLAUSE   TIME CLAUSE
> Sandra was surprised *when she opened her e-mail.*
>
> MAIN CLAUSE   TIME CLAUSE
> Sandra began to think *after she put the phone down.*

🌐 Time clauses are more common after the main clause.

> MAIN CLAUSE   TIME CLAUSE
> They canceled the card *before the criminals used it.*

2.3 Ordering Events

A *When* means "at almost the same time." Use *when* to introduce the first event.

> FIRST EVENT   SECOND EVENT
> *When* Sandra opened her e-mail, she was surprised.
>
> SECOND EVENT   FIRST EVENT
> Sandra called the number *when* she got home.

B Use *after* to introduce the first event.

> FIRST EVENT   SECOND EVENT
> *After* Sandra put the phone down, she began to think.
>
> SECOND EVENT   FIRST EVENT
> She felt much better *after* she called the bank.

C Use *before* to introduce the second event.

> FIRST EVENT   SECOND EVENT
> She canceled the card *before* they used it.
>
> SECOND EVENT   FIRST EVENT
> *Before* they sent her prize, they asked her to pay a fee.

D *Before* and *after* are also prepositions. You can use them before nouns that do not have verbs after them.

> *After work,* she went home.
> She was so excited *before the phone call.*

⌨ Grammar Application

Exercise 2.1 *When, Before,* or *After?*

A Choose the correct words to complete the sentences about the article.

1 Sandra opened her e-mail (**when**)/ **before** she got to work.
2 **When / Before** she read the e-mail, Sandra was surprised.
3 She called the number **after / before** she got home.

4 The man and Sandra talked **before/after** he had her personal bank information.

5 **When/Before** Sandra said she didn't have $1,000, the man asked for her credit card number.

6 She gave him her address **after/before** she read out her credit card number.

7 **After/Before** she put the phone down, Sandra realized her mistake.

8 She called her credit card company **before/after** she spoke to the man.

B Pair Work Compare your answers with a partner. Which sentences can use both words?

Exercise 2.2 Ordering Events

A Listen to the story about another scam. Number the pictures in the order the events happened.

a _____

He bought a newspaper.

b _____

_____

c _____

_____

d _____

_____

e ___1___

_____

f _____

_____

B Write the sentences under the correct pictures in A.

He bought a newspaper.

He read an e-mail from the bank.

He met a co-worker on the train.

He left for work.

He wrote a note to his wife.

He called his wife.

C Complete the story with *when, before,* and *after*. Then listen again to check your answers.

About a year ago, my friend Leo was almost a scam victim. One morning, he saw an e-mail from his bank _*before*_ he went to work. (1) _____ he opened the e-mail, (2) it said, "You have a new account number. Write your old account number here so we can check your identity." He didn't have time to reply _____ he left home. (3) _____ he left for work, he wrote (4) a note to his wife, "Please reply to the bank's e-mail." Then he left for work.

_____ he got to the subway station, he bought a newspaper. (5) _____ he got on the train, he met a co-worker and they talked. (6) _____ he read the newspaper at lunchtime, he read an article about a bank (7) Internet scam. He realized the e-mail from the bank was that scam. _____ he (8) read the article, he called his wife. Luckily, _____ his wife read the e-mail, she (9) realized it was a scam and deleted the e-mail.

Exercise 2.3 Writing Main Clauses and Time Clauses

A Over to You **What did you do yesterday? Complete each sentence by adding a main clause with a subject and a verb. For sentences with the time clause first, use a comma.**

1 _____ before I left home yesterday morning.

2 After I ate lunch _____ .

3 Before I went home last night _____ .

4 _____ when I got home last night.

5 _____ after I ate dinner.

6 Before I went to bed _____ .

B Over to You **What did you do today? Complete each sentence by adding a time clause with *when*, *before*, or *after*. For sentences with the time clause first, use a comma.**

1 I got dressed _____ .

2 _____ I brushed my teeth.

3 I left the house / apartment _____ .

4 I got to school _____ .

5 _____ I went to the classroom.

6 _____ my English class started.

C Pair Work **Share your sentences with a partner. Did you do any of the same things?**

Exercise 2.4 More Main Clauses and Time Clauses

Pair Work **Tell a story about a scam from this unit or use your own ideas. First make notes to help you. Then share your story with a partner. Ask questions about your partner's scam story.**

A *This happened to a friend last year. When she checked her e-mail, she saw a message from a stranger.*

B *What did it say?*

3 Avoid Common Mistakes ⚠

1 **Check the spelling of *when*, *before*, and *after*.**

When
~~Whin~~ she read the e-mail, she got excited.   They canceled the card ~~befor~~ *before* the criminals used it.

after
She thought about it ~~affter~~ she put the phone down.

2 **When the time clause comes first, use a comma. Don't use a comma when the main clause comes first.**

When she got home⌄she called the company.   She called the company / when she got home.

3 **Don't forget the subject in the main clause and the time clause.**

she
Before Ana called the company,⌄checked the address.

Ana
Before⌄called the company, she checked the address.

Editing Task

Find and correct 13 more mistakes in this story about a scam.

When﹢got home one night two months ago I had a voice mail message.
When I listened to the message, got excited. The message said, "Congratulations.
You are a winner in our contest." Befor I made dinner, called the number.
A woman said, "We called you two weeks ago, but you didn't answer. Please hold."
5 After waited for an hour, I put the phone down.

Whin my wife got home I asked her, "Did you get a message about a prize
drawing?" She said, "Yes, but afther heard it, I deleted it. It's a scam." When she
said that I didn't say anything.

I realized my mistake, when we got the phone bill four days later. When read
10 the bill I didn't believe it. That one-hour call cost $5,000!

4 Academic Writing

Narrative Paragraph

Brainstorm > Organize > Write > Edit

In Unit 14, you answered the prompt below. In this unit (15), you will learn how to add variety to your writing. Then you will review, revise, and edit your narrative paragraph.

> *Write a paragraph about the history of a business.*

Using Past Time Clauses

Good writers use a variety of ways to show relationships between events. In addition to time-order transition signals, writers can use **past time clauses** with *when*, *before*, and *after* to show the sequence of events. Use a comma (,) after past time clauses that come at the beginning of a sentence.

time-order transition signal

In 1995, Larry Page and Sergey Brin were students at Stanford University. They met **when Larry was 22 and Sergey was 21**.

past time clause

time-order transition signal   past time clause

Google bought YouTube **in 2006**. **After YouTube became a part of Google**, the company still planned to operate independently.

My Writing

Exercise 4.1 Applying the Skill

Look at the first draft of your paragraph on page 183. Combine some of your sentences or add new ideas using past time clauses with *when*, *before*, or *after*.

_____

_____

_____

_____

_____

_____

_____

_____

Exercise 4.2 Revising Your Ideas

1 Work with a partner. Use the questions below to give feedback on the ideas in your partner's paragraph.

  • Which details in your partner's paragraph are the most interesting?
  • Which details in your partner's paragraph are unnecessary?
  • What types of details could your partner add to make the paragraph more interesting?

2 Make any necessary changes to your paragraph.

Exercise 4.3 Editing Your Writing

Use the checklist to review and edit your paragraph.

Did you write a narrative paragraph about the history of a business?	
Did you write about four important events in chronoligcal order?	
Did you give the date or time when these events happened?	
Did you add details to these main events?	
Did you use the correct forms of the simple past?	
Did you include some time-order transition signals?	
Did you add variety to your writing with past time clauses?	

Exercise 4.4 Writing Your Final Draft

Apply the feedback and edits from Exercises 4.2 and 4.3 to write the final draft of your paragraphs.

Appendices

1 Capitalization and Punctuation Rules

Capitalize	Examples
1 The first letter of the first word of a sentence	*Today is a great day.*
2 The pronoun *I*	*Yesterday I went to hear a new rock band.*
3 Names of people	*Simón Bolívar, Joseph Chung*
4 Names of buildings, streets, geographic locations, and organizations	*Taj Majal, Broadway, Mt. Everest, United Nations*
5 Titles of people	*Dr., Mr., Mrs., Ms.*
6 Days, months, and holidays	*Tuesday, April, Valentine's Day*
7 Names of courses or classes	*Biology 101, English Composition II*
8 Titles of books, movies, and plays	*Crime and Punishment, Avatar, Hamlet*
9 States, countries, languages, and nationalities	*California, Mexico, Spanish, South Korean, Canadian*
10 Names of religions	*Hinduism, Catholicism, Islam, Judaism*

Punctuation	Examples
1 Use a period (.) at the end of a sentence.	*He is Korean.*
2 Use a question mark (?) at the end of a question.	*Do you want to buy a car?*
3 Use an exclamation point (!) to show strong emotion (e.g., surprise, anger, shock).	*Wait! I'm not ready yet. I can't believe it!*

4 Use an apostrophe (') for possessive nouns.
    Add 's for singular nouns.
    Add s' for plural nouns.
    Add 's for irregular plural nouns.
    Use an apostrophe (') for contractions.
	
	That's Sue's umbrella.
	Those are the students' books. BUT
	Bring me the children's shoes.
	I'll be back next week. He can't drive a car.

5 Use a comma (,):
  • between words in a series of three or more items. (Place *and* before the last item.)
  • before *and, or, but,* and *so* to connect two complete sentences.
	
	I like fish, chicken, turkey, and mashed potatoes.
	You can watch TV, but I have to study for a test.

2 Spelling Rules for Noun Plurals

1	Add -s to most singular nouns to form plural nouns.	*a camera – two cameras* *a key – keys*	*a model – two models* *a student – students*
2	Add -es to nouns that end in -ch, -sh, -ss, and -x.	*watch – watches* *class – classes*	*dish – dishes* *tax – taxes*
3	With nouns that end in a consonant + -y, change the y to i and add -es.	*accessory – accessories*	*battery – batteries*
4	With nouns that end in -ife, change the ending to -ives.	*knife – knives* *wife – wives*	*life – lives*
5	Add -es to nouns that end in -o after a consonant. **Exception:** Add -s only to nouns that end in -o and refer to music.	*potato – potatoes* *piano – pianos*	*tomato – tomatoes* *soprano – sopranos*
6	Add -s to nouns that end in -o after a vowel.	*radio – radios*	*shampoo – shampoos*
7	Some plural nouns have irregular forms. These are the most common irregular plural nouns in academic writing.	*man – men* *child – children* *foot – feet*	*woman – women* *person – people* *tooth – teeth*
8	Some nouns have the same form for singular and plural.	*one deer – two deer* *one fish – two fish*	*one sheep – two sheep*
9	Some nouns are only plural. They do not have a singular form.	*clothes* *glasses* *headphones* *jeans*	*pants* *scissors* *sunglasses*

3 Verb Forms

Present: *Be*

Affirmative Statements

SINGULAR		
Subject	*Be*	
I	**am**	late.
You	**are**	
He She It	**is**	difficult.

PLURAL		
Subject	*Be*	
We You They	**are**	from Seoul.

Negative Statements

SINGULAR		
Subject	*Be + Not*	
I	**am not**	in class.
You	**are not**	
He She It	**is not**	

PLURAL		
Subject	*Be + Not*	
We You They	**are not**	students.

Affirmative Contractions

SINGULAR

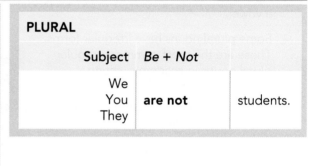

I am → I**'m**
You are → You**'re**
He is → He**'s**
Jun-Ho is → Jun-Ho**'s**
She is → She**'s**
His mother is → His mother**'s**
It is → It**'s**
My name is → My name**'s**

PLURAL

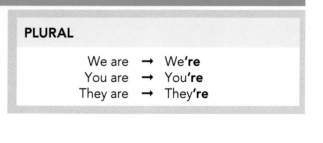

We are → We**'re**
You are → You**'re**
They are → They**'re**

Negative Contractions

SINGULAR

I am not	→	I**'m not**
You are not	→	You**'re not** / You **aren't**
He is not	→	He**'s not** / He **isn't**
She is not	→	She**'s not** / She **isn't**
It is not	→	It**'s not** / It **isn't**

PLURAL

We are not	→	We**'re not** / We **aren't**
You are not	→	You**'re not** / You **aren't**
They are not	→	They**'re not** / They **aren't**

Singular Yes/No Questions

Be	Subject	
Am	I	
Are	you	in class?
Is	he she it	

Singular Short Answers

AFFIRMATIVE

	Subject	*Be*
Yes,	I	**am**.
	you	**are**.
	he she it	**is**.

NEGATIVE

	Subject	*Be + Not*
No,	I	**am not**.
	you	**are not**.
	he she it	**is not**.

Plural Yes/No Questions

Be	Subject	
Are	we you they	late?

Plural Short Answers

AFFIRMATIVE

	Subject	*Be*
Yes,	we you they	**are**.

NEGATIVE

	Subject	*Be + Not*
No,	we you they	**are not**.

Negative Short Answer Contractions

SINGULAR

No, I am not.	→	No, I**'m not**.
No, you are not.	→	No, you**'re not**. No, you **aren't**.
No, he is not.	→	No, he**'s not**. No, he **isn't**.
No, she is not.	→	No, she**'s not**. No, she **isn't**.
No, it is not.	→	No, it**'s not**. No, it **isn't**.

PLURAL

No, we are not.	→	No, we**'re not**. No, we **aren't**.
No, you are not.	→	No, you**'re not**. No, you **aren't**.
No, they are not.	→	No, they**'re not**. No, they **aren't**.

Information Questions

SINGULAR SUBJECTS

Wh- Word	Be	Subject
Who		your teacher?
What		your major?
When	is	our exam?
Where		the building?
How		your class?

PLURAL SUBJECTS

Wh- Word	Be	Subject
Who		your teachers?
What		your plans?
When	are	your exams?
Where		your books?
How		your classes?

Contractions with Singular Subjects

SINGULAR

Who is	→	**Who's**
What is	→	**What's**
When is	→	**When's**
Where is	→	**Where's**
How is	→	**How's**

There Is / There Are

Affirmative Statements

There	Be	Subject	Place / Time
There	is	a parking lot a free tour	on Alameda Street. at 10:00.
	are	a lot of little shops free tours	in the area. on most days.

Contraction

There is → There's

Negative Statements

There	Be + Not / No	Subject	Place / Time
There	isn't is no	a bank bank	in Union Station.
	isn't is no	a show show	at 8:00.
There	's no	bank	in Union Station.
		show	at 8:00.
There	aren't are no	any cars cars	on Olvera Street.
	aren't are no	any tours tours	in the evening.

Yes / No Questions and Short Answers

Be	There	Subject	Place / Time
Is	there	a visitor's center	on Olvera Street?
		a performance	at 6:00?
Are		any parking lots	in the area?
		any tours	in the evening?

Short Answers

Yes, **there is**.

No, **there isn't**.

Yes, **there are**.

No, **there aren't**.

Simple Present

Affirmative Statements

SINGULAR

Subject	Verb	
I You	**eat**	vegetables every day.
He She It	**eats**	

PLURAL

Subject	Verb	
We You They	**have**	many friends.

Negative Statements

SINGULAR

Subject	Do / Does + Not	Base Form of Verb	
I You	**do not** **don't**	**eat**	a lot of meat.
He She It	**does not** **doesn't**		

PLURAL

Subject	Do + Not	Base Form of Verb	
We You They	**do not** **don't**	**exercise**	in the morning.

Yes / No Questions

Do / Does	Subject	Base Form of Verb	
Do	I you we they	**fall asleep**	in 30 minutes?
Does	he she it		

AFFIRMATIVE			
Yes	Subject	*Do / Does*	
Yes,	I you we they	**do.**	
	he she it	**does.**	

NEGATIVE			
No	Subject	*Do / Does + Not*	
No,	I you we they	**do not.** **don't.**	
	he she it	**does not.** **doesn't.**	

Wh- word	*Do / Does*	Subject	Base Form of Verb	
Who	do	I you we they	**see**	at school?
What			**eat**	at parties?
When			**celebrate**	that holiday?
Where	does	he she it	**study**	for school?
Why			**live**	at home?
How			**meet**	new people?

Present Progressive

Subject	*Be*	Verb + *-ing*
I	**am**	
You We They	**are**	**talking.**
He She It	**is**	

Contractions	
I am	→ **I'm**
You are	→ You**'re**
We are	→ We**'re**
They are	→ They**'re**
He is	→ He**'s**
She is	→ She**'s**
It is	→ It**'s**

Negative Statements

Subject	Be + Not	Verb + -ing
I	am not	
You We They	are not	talking.
He She It	is not	

Contractions

I am not	→ I**'m not**	
You are not	→ You**'re not**	You **aren't**
We are not	→ We**'re not**	We **aren't**
They are not	→ They**'re not**	They **aren't**
He is not	→ He**'s not**	He **isn't**
She is not	→ She**'s not**	She **isn't**
It is not	→ It**'s not**	It **isn't**

Yes/No Questions

Be	Subject	Verb + -ing
Am	I	
Are	you we they	working?
Is	he she it	

Short Answers

AFFIRMATIVE	NEGATIVE	
Yes, I **am**.	No, I**'m not**.	
Yes, you **are**.	No, you**'re not**.	No, you **aren't**.
Yes, we **are**.	No, we**'re not**.	No, we **aren't**.
Yes, they **are**.	No, they**'re not**.	No, they **aren't**.
Yes, he **is**.	No, he**'s not**.	No, he **isn't**.
Yes, she **is**.	No, she**'s not**.	No, she **isn't**.
Yes, it **is**.	No, it**'s not**.	No, it **isn't**.

Information Questions

Wh- Word	Be	Subject	Verb + -ing
Who	am	I	hearing?
What		you we they	studying?
When	are		leaving?
Where			going?
Why	is	he she it	laughing?
How			feeling?

Wh- Word as Subject	Be	Verb + -ing
Who	is	talking?
What		happening?

Simple Past: *Be*

AFFIRMATIVE				NEGATIVE			
Subject	*Was / Were*			Subject	*Was / Were + Not*		
I He She It	**was**	in the computer lab.		I He She It	**was not** **wasn't**	in class.	
We You They	**were**			We You They	**were not** **weren't**		

Yes/ No Questions

Was / Were	Subject	
Was	I he she it	very smart?
Were	we you they	in college?

Short Answers

AFFIRMATIVE				NEGATIVE			
Yes	Subject	*Was / Were*		No	Subject	*Was / Were + Not*	
Yes,	I he she it	**was.**		**No,**	I he she it	**was not.** **wasn't.**	
	we you they	**were.**			we you they	**were not.** **weren't.**	

Information Questions

Wh- Word	*Was / Were*	Subject	
Who	**was**	your best friend	as a child?
What		your favorite class	last semester?
When		her birthday party?	
What time		the meeting	on Monday?
Where	**were**	his partners?	
Why		they	successful?
How		the concerts	the other night?
How old		their cars	in 2011?

Simple Past

AFFIRMATIVE

Subject	Simple Past Verb	
I You We They He She It	**started**	in 1962.

NEGATIVE

Subject	*Did + Not*	Base Form of Verb	
I You We They He She It	**did not didn't**	**sign**	a contract.

Yes/No Questions

Did	Subject	Base Form of Verb	
Did	I you we they he she it	**finish**	the report?

Short Answers

AFFIRMATIVE

Yes	Subject	*Did*
Yes,	I you we they he she it	**did.**

NEGATIVE

No	Subject	*Did + Not*
No,	I you we they he she it	**did not. didn't.**

Information Questions

Wh- Word	*Did*	Subject	Base Form of Verb	
Who			**write**	about?
What		I you we they he she it	**do**	yesterday?
When	**did**		**finish**	our report?
Where			**visit**	on vacation?
Why			**start**	a company?
How			**save**	enough money?

Past Progressive

Statements

AFFIRMATIVE

Subject	Past of *Be*	Verb + *-ing*
I He She It	**was**	**working.**
You We They	**were**	

NEGATIVE

Subject	Past of *Be* + *Not*	Verb + *-ing*
I He She It	**was not / wasn't**	**working.**
You We They	**were not / weren't**	

Yes/No Questions

Past of *Be*	Subject	Verb + *-ing*
Was	I he she it	**working?**
Were	you we they	**working?**

Short Answers

AFFIRMATIVE

	Subject	Past of *Be*
Yes,	I he she it	**was.**
	you we they	**were.**

NEGATIVE

	Subject	Past of *Be* + *Not*
No,	I he she it	**were not. weren't.**
	you we they	**were not. weren't.**

Information Questions

Wh- Word	Past of *Be*	Subject	Verb + *-ing*
Who	**was**	I he she it	**studying?**
What			**doing?**
When			**researching?**
Where	**were**	you we they	**working?**
Why			**experimenting?**
How			**feeling?**

Wh- Word as Subject	Past of *Be*	Verb + *-ing*
Who	**was**	**talking?**
What	**was**	**happening?**

Future: *Be Going To*

AFFIRMATIVE

Subject	Be	Going To	Base Form of Verb	
I	am			
You We They	are	going to	get	a job.
He She It	is			

NEGATIVE

Subject	Be + Not	Going To	Base Form of Verb	
I	am not			
You We They	are not	going to	get	a job.
He She It	is not			

Yes/No Questions

Be	Subject	Going To	Base Form of Verb	
Am	I			
Are	you we they	going to	get	a job?
Is	he she it			

Short Answers

AFFIRMATIVE

	Subject	Be
Yes,	I	am.
	you we they	are.
	he she it	is.

NEGATIVE

	Subject	Be + Not
No,	I	'm not.
	you we they	aren't.
	he she it	isn't.

Information Questions

Wh- Word	Be	Subject	Going To	Base Form of Verb	
Who	Am	I		interview	tomorrow?
What		you we they		do	after graduation?
When	Are			leave	for New York?
Where			going to	work	after college?
Why	Is	he she it		move	to Canada?
How				pay	his loans?

Wh- Word as Subject	Be	Going To	Base Form of Verb	
Who	is	going to	get	a job after college?
What			happen	after school?

Future: *Will*

Statements

AFFIRMATIVE

Subject	Will	Base Form of Verb	
I You We They He She It	will 'll	have	a healthy life.

NEGATIVE

Subject	Will + Not	Base Form of Verb	
I You We They He She It	will not won't	have	a healthy life.

Yes/No Questions

Will	Subject	Base Form of Verb	
Will	I you we they he she it	have	a healthy life?

Short Answers

AFFIRMATIVE

Yes, I Yes, you Yes, we Yes, they Yes, he Yes, she Yes, it	will.

NEGATIVE

No, I No, you No, we No, they No, he No, she No, it	won't.

Information Questions

Wh- Word	Will	Subject	Base Form of Verb	
Who			meet	at the interview tomorrow?
What			do	in your training program?
When		I you we they he she it	return	your documents?
Where	will		find	information about careers?
Why			travel	to South America?
How			build	new apartments?

Imperatives

Statements

AFFIRMATIVE	
Base Form of Verb	
Smile	and be helpful.
Look	at people when you talk to them.

NEGATIVE		
Do + Not	**Base Form of Verb**	
Don't/ Do not	**interrupt**	people who are very busy.
	do	this in the beginning.

4 Common Regular and Irregular Verbs

Regular		Irregular	
Base Form	**Past Form**	**Base Form**	**Past Form**
call	called	come	came
decide	decided	do	did
happen	happened	get	got
like	liked	go	went
live	lived	have	had
look	looked	make	made
move	moved	put	put
start	started	read	read
talk	talked	say	said
try	tried	see	saw
work	worked		

5 Irregular Verbs

Base Form	Simple Past
be	was / were
become	became
begin	began
bite	bit
blow	blew
break	broke
bring	brought
build	built
buy	bought
catch	caught
choose	chose
come	came
cost	cost
cut	cut
do	did
draw	drew
drink	drank
drive	drove
eat	ate
fall	fell
feed	fed
feel	felt
fight	fought
find	found
fly	flew
forget	forgot
forgive	forgave
get	got
give	gave
go	went
grow	grew
have	had
hear	heard
hide	hid
hit	hit
hold	held
hurt	hurt

Base Form	Simple Past
keep	kept
know	knew
leave	left
lose	lost
make	made
meet	met
pay	paid
put	put
read	read
ride	rode
run	ran
say	said
see	saw
sell	sold
send	sent
set	set
shake	shook
show	showed
shut	shut
sing	sang
sit	sat
sleep	slept
speak	spoke
spend	spent
stand	stood
steal	stole
swim	swam
take	took
teach	taught
tell	told
think	thought
throw	threw
understand	understood
wake	woke
wear	wore
win	won
write	wrote

6 Spelling Rules for Possessive Nouns

1 Add 's to singular nouns to show possession.	*The manager's name is Mr. Patel.* (one manager) *The boss's ideas are helpful.* (one boss)
2 Add an apostrophe (') to plural nouns ending in -s to show possession.	*The managers' names are hard to remember.* (more than one manager) *The bosses' ideas are very good.* (more than one boss)
3 For irregular plural nouns, add 's to show possession.	*The men's uniforms are heavy.* (more than one man) *The children's room is messy.* (more than one child)
4 *My, your, his, her, our,* and *their* can come before a possessive noun.	*My friend's sister is in Peru.* *Our parents' names are short.*

7 Noncount Nouns and Containers

Common Noncount Nouns

Food and Liquids		Materials	School Subjects	Weather	Other
beef	rice	leather	algebra	fog	advice
bread	salt	metal	art	ice	furniture
butter	seafood	oil	biology	rain	garbage
cheese	shrimp	plastic	economics	snow	help
coffee	soup	silk	English	weather	homework
fish	spinach	wood	geography		information
ice cream	sugar		history		jewelry
meat	tea		music		mail
milk	water		physics		money
olive oil			psychology		noise
			science		traffic
					vocabulary
					work

Measurement Words and Containers

a bag of potatoes rice	**a bowl** of soup pasta	**a glass** of water soda	**a piece** of cake meat
a bar of chocolate soap	**a bunch** of grapes bananas	**a head** of lettuce cabbage	**a plate** of eggs chicken
a bottle of oil ketchup	**a can** of beans tuna	**a jar** of mustard pickles	**a pound** of butter cheese
a box of cereal candy	**a carton** of milk juice	**a loaf** of bread	**a slice** of pie pizza

8 Metric Conversion

1 ounce = 28 grams 1 gram = .04 ounce	1 mile = 1.6 kilometers 1 kilometer = .62 mile
1 pound = .45 kilogram 1 kilogram = 2.2 pounds	1 foot = .30 meter 1 meter = 3.3 feet
1 liter = .26 gallon 1 gallon = 3.8 liters	1 inch = 2.54 centimeters 1 centimeter = .39 inch

9 Subject and Object Pronouns

Subject Pronoun	Possessive Adjective	Object Pronoun	
I	my	me	I can't find the calculator. My desk is so messy. My boss is unhappy with me.
you	your	you	You are very organized. Your desk is so neat. I want to be like you.
he	his	him	He is a new employee. His old job was in Hong Kong. This is very exciting to him.
she	her	her	She went home. Her computer is off. I'll call her.
it	its	it	It's a new company. Its president is Mr. Janesh. He wants it to be successful.
we	our	us	We are looking for the reports. Our boss wants to read them. The reports are important to us.
they	their	them	They are writing a report. Their team members will help them.

10 Indefinite and Definite Articles

Indefinite Article

1	Use *a/an* with singular count nouns.	*She made a decision about her job.* *An analyst examines something in detail.*
2	Use *a* when the noun begins with a consonant sound.	*She made a decision about her job.*
3	Use *an* when the noun begins with a vowel sound.	*An analyst examines something in detail.*
4	Use *a* before adjectives or adverbs that begin with a consonant sound.	*Tony found a great apartment in Chicago.*
5	Use *a* before words that begin with *u* when the *u* makes a "you" sound.	*James went to a university in Boston.* *The economy is a universal concern.*
6	Use *a/an* to introduce a person or thing for the first time to a listener. When you mention the person or thing again, use *the*.	*Tom bought a car.* (The listener does not know about this car.) *The car was not very expensive.* (Now the listener knows about this car.)

Definite Article

1	You can use *the* before singular or plural count nouns, and before noncount nouns.	*The job is a good one.* *The choices were interesting.* *The information is very useful.*
2	Use *the* to talk about people or things that both the listener and speaker know about.	*The president discussed the plan.* (Everyone knows the president and the plan.) *The moon and the stars were beautiful last night.* (Everyone knows the moon and the stars.)
3	Use *the* to talk about a specific noun.	*"The teacher gave us difficult homework tonight."* (The speaker and listener know this teacher.) *"The game was interesting." "I agree."* (The speaker and listener are thinking of the same game.)

11 Spelling Rules for Verbs Ending in *-ing*

1 For most verbs, add *-ing**.

go → going   say → saying   talk → talking

2 If the verb ends in a silent *-e*, delete *e* and add *-ing*.

live → living   make → making   write → writing

3 For *be* and *see*, don't drop the *e* because it is not silent.

be → being   see → seeing

4 If the verb ends in *-ie*, change the *ie* to *y* and add *-ing*.

die → dying   lie → lying

5 If the verb has one syllable and follows the pattern consonant, vowel, consonant (CVC), double the last letter and add *-ing*.

get → getting   put → putting   sit → sitting

6 Do not double the consonant if the verb ends in *-w, -x,* or *-y*.

grow → growing   fix → fixing   say → saying

7 If the verb has two syllables, ends in the pattern CVC, and is stressed on the last syllable, double the last letter and add *-ing*.

beGIN → beginning

8 If the verb has two syllables and is stressed on the first syllable, do not double the last letter.

LISten → listening   TRAVel → traveling   VISit → visiting

* Verbs that end in *-ing* are also called *gerunds* when they are used as a noun. The same spelling rules above apply to gerunds as well.

12 Spelling and Pronunciation Rules for Simple Present

Spelling of Third-Person Singular Verbs

1 Add *-s* to most verbs.
Add *-s* to verbs ending in a vowel* + *-y*.

drinks, rides, runs, sees, sleeps   buys, pays, says

2 Add *-es* to verbs ending in *-ch, -sh, -ss, -x*.
Add *-es* to verbs ending in a consonant** + *-o*.

teaches, pushes, misses, fixes   does, goes

3 For verbs that end in a consonant + *-y*, change the *y* to *i* and add *-es*.

cry → cries   study → studies

4 Some verbs are irregular.

be → am / are / is   have → has

  * **Vowels:** the letters *a, e, i, o, u*
** **Consonants:** the letters *b, c, d, f, g, h, j, k, l, m, n, p, q, r, s, t, v, w, x, y, z*

Pronunciation of Third-Person Singular Verbs

1 Say /s/ after /f/, /k/, /p/, and /t/ sounds.
laughs, drinks, walks, sleeps, writes, gets

2 Say /z/ after /b/, /d/, /g/, /v/, /m/, /n/, /l/, and /r/ sounds and all vowel sounds.
grabs, rides, hugs, lives, comes, runs, smiles, hears, sees, plays, buys, goes, studies

3 Say /əz/ after /tʃ/, /ʃ/, /s/, /ks/, /z/, and /dʒ/ sounds.
teaches, pushes, kisses, fixes, uses, changes

4 Pronounce the vowel sound in *does* and *says* differently from *do* and *say*.
do /du:/ → *does* /dʌz/   *say* /seɪ/ → *says* /sez/

13 Spelling and Pronunciation Rules for Regular Verbs in Simple Past

Spelling of Regular Verbs

1 For most verbs, add *-ed*.	*work* → *worked*
2 For verbs ending in *-e*, add *-d*.	*live* → *lived*
3 For verbs ending in consonant + *-y*, change the *y* to *i* and add *-ed*.	*study* → *studied*
4 For verbs ending in vowel + *-y*, add *-ed*.	*play* → *played*
5 For one-syllable verbs ending in consonant-vowel-consonant (CVC), double the consonant.	*plan* → *planned*
6 Do not double the consonant if the verb ends in *-x* or *-w*.	*show* → *showed*
7 For two-syllable verbs ending in CVC and stressed on the first syllable, do not double the consonant.	*TRAvel* → *TRAveled*
8 For two-syllable verbs ending in CVC and stressed on the second syllable, double the consonant.	*conTROL* → *conTROLLED*

Pronunciation of Regular Verbs

1 When the verb ends in /t/ or /d/, say *-ed* as /ɪd/ or /əd/.	*wait* → *waited*	*decide* → *decided*
2 When the verb ends in /f/, /k/, /p/, /s/, /ʃ/, and /tʃ/, say *-ed* as /t/.	*laugh* → *laughed* *look* → *looked* *stop* → *stopped*	*miss* → *missed* *finish* → *finished* *watch* → *watched*
3 For verbs that end in other consonant and vowel sounds, say *-ed* as /d/.	*agree* → *agreed* *borrow* → *borrowed* *change* → *changed*	*listen* → *listened* *live* → *lived* *play* → *played*

14 Adjectives and Adverbs: Comparative and Superlative Forms

	Adjective	Comparative	Superlative
1 One-Syllable Adjectives			
a Add -er and -est to one-syllable adjectives.	cheap new old small strong tall young	cheaper newer older smaller stronger taller younger	the cheapest the newest the oldest the smallest the strongest the tallest the youngest
b If the adjective ends with one vowel + one consonant, double the last letter and add -er or -est. Do not double the consonant w.	big hot sad thin	bigger hotter sadder thinner	the biggest the hottest the saddest the thinnest
2 Two-Syllable Adjectives			
a Add more or the most to most two-syllable adjectives.	boring famous handsome patient	more boring more famous more handsome more patient	the most boring the most famous the most handsome the most patient
b Some two-syllable adjectives have two forms.	narrow simple	narrower / more narrow simpler / more simple	the narrowest / the most narrow the simplest / the most simple
c If the adjective has two syllables and ends in -y, change the y to i and add -er or -est.	angry easy friendly happy lucky pretty silly	angrier easier friendlier happier luckier prettier sillier	the angriest the easiest the friendliest the happiest the luckiest the prettiest the silliest

	Adjective	Comparative	Superlative
3 Three-or-More-Syllable Adjectives Add *more* or *the most* to adjectives with three or more syllables.	beautiful difficult enjoyable expensive important serious	more beautiful more difficult more enjoyable more expensive more important more serious	the most beautiful the most difficult the most enjoyable the most expensive the most important the most serious
4 Irregular Adjectives Some adjectives have irregular forms.	bad far good	worse farther / further better	the worst the farthest / the furthest the best

	Adjective	Comparative	Superlative
1 -ly Adverbs Most adverbs end in *-ly*.	patiently quickly quietly slowly	more patiently more quickly more quietly more slowly	(the) most patiently (the) most quickly (the) most quietly (the) most slowly
2 One-Syllable Adverbs A few adverbs do not end in *-ly*. Add *-er* and *-est* to these adverbs.	fast hard	faster harder	(the) fastest (the) hardest
3 Irregular Adverbs Some adverbs have irregular forms.	badly far well	worse farther / further better	(the) worst (the) farthest / furthest (the) best

People usually only use *the* with superlative adverbs in formal writing and speaking.

15 Adverbs with -*ly*

Adjective	Adverb	Adjective	Adverb
bad	badly	loud	loudly
beautiful	beautifully	nervous	nervously
careful	carefully	nice	nicely
clear	clearly	patient	patiently
close	closely	polite	politely
confident	confidently	proper	properly
deep	deeply	quick	quickly
fluent	fluently	quiet	quietly
honest	honestly	slow	slowly
interesting	interestingly	strong	strongly
late	lately		

Spelling Rules for Adverbs

		Adjectives	Adverbs
1	After most adjectives, add -*ly*.	accidental interesting nice peaceful	accidentally interestingly nicely peacefully
2	After -*y*, delete *y* and add -*ily*.	easy happy	easily happily
3	After -*ic*, add -*ally*.	automatic terrific	automatically terrifically
4	After a consonant + -*le*, drop the *e* and add -*y*.	gentle terrible	gently terribly

16 Modal Verbs and Modal-like Expressions

Modals are helper verbs. Most modals have multiple meanings.

Function	Modal Verb	Time	Example
Ability	can	present	I can speak three languages.
	could	past	She couldn't attend class yesterday.
	be able to	present, past	I'm not able to help you tomorrow.
	know how to	present, past	I know how to speak two languages.
Possibility	can	present	I can meet you at 3:00 for coffee.
	could	past	People could read the newspaper online many years ago.
Requests less formal	can	present, future	Can you stop that noise now?
more formal	could would	present, future	Could you turn off your cell phone, please? Would you please come to my party?
Permission less formal	can could	present, future	You can give me your answer next week. Yes, you could watch TV now.
more formal	may	present, future	You may leave now.
Advice	should ought to might want to	present, future	What should you do if you live in a noisy place? You really ought to save your money. You might want to wait until next month.
Suggestions	Why don't Let's	present, future	Why don't we study together? Let's read the chapter together.
Necessity	have to need to must	past, present, future	We had to cancel our date at the last minute. She needs to make a schedule. All students must send their applications out on time.
Conclusion	must	present, future	Today is Monday, so tomorrow must be Tuesday.

17 Stative (Non-Action) Verbs

1 Stative verbs describe states, not actions. These are stative verbs: *love, know, want, need, seem, mean,* and *agree*. Use the simple present with stative verbs, not the present progressive.	*I don't like rude people.* NOT ~~I'm not liking~~ *rude people.* *What do you know about this?* NOT *What* ~~are you knowing~~? *They seem upset.* NOT *They* ~~are seeming~~ *upset.* *Experts don't agree on the meaning of some gestures.* NOT *Experts* ~~are not agreeing~~ *on the meaning of some gestures.*
2 Some verbs have a stative meaning and an action meaning.	STATIVE *I think grammar is fun.* (= an opinion) ACTION *I'm thinking about my homework.* (= using my mind) STATIVE *The book looks interesting.* (= appears) ACTION *We're looking at the book right now.* (= using our eyes) STATIVE *Do you have a dog?* (= own) ACTION *Are you having a good time?* (= experiencing)
3 You can use *feel* with the same meaning in the simple present and the present progressive.	*I feel tired today.* OR *I'm feeling tired today.* *How do you feel?* OR *How are you feeling?*

18 Verbs + Gerunds and Infinitives

Verbs Followed by a Gerund Only

admit	keep (= continue)
avoid	mind (= object to)
consider	miss
delay	postpone
deny	practice
discuss	quit
enjoy	recall (= remember)
finish	risk
imagine	suggest
involve	understand

Verbs Followed by an Infinitive Only

afford	help	pretend
agree	hope	promise
arrange	intend	refuse
attempt	learn	seem
decide	manage	tend (= be likely)
deserve	need	threaten
expect	offer	volunteer
fail	plan	want
forget	prepare	

Verbs Followed by a Gerund or an Infinitive

begin	like	start
continue	love	
hate	prefer	

Index

Art Credits

Acknowledgements

The authors and publishers acknowledge the following sources of copyright material and are grateful for the permissions granted. While every effort has been made, it has not always been possible to identify the sources of all the material used, or to trace all copyright holders. If any omissions are brought to our notice, we will be happy to include the appropriate acknowledgements on reprinting and in the next update to the digital edition, as applicable.

Key: U = Unit

Photography

All the photos are sourced from Getty Images.

U1: Hero Images; 7postman/iStock/Getty Images Plus; Bobby Coutu/E+; Ajr_images/iStock/Getty Images Plus; Cunfek/iStock; Assembly/DigitalVision; Spaces Images/ Blend Images; Aliraza Khatri's Photography/Moment; Franck-Boston/iStock/Getty Images Plus; Fatboy129/ iStock/Getty Images Plus; We Are/DigitalVision; Wavebreakmedia Ltd/Wavebreak Media; **U2**: Bonfanti Diego/Image Source; Andr Adami/EyeEm; Westend61; GrapeImages/E+; Jeremyiswild/iStock/Getty Images Plus; lvcandy/DigitalVision Vectors; Bernd Thissen/DPA; Reimphoto/iStock Editorial; **U3**: MirageC/Moment; Nathan Griffith/Corbis Documentary; Justin Sullivan; Seyfettinozel/iStock/Getty Images Plus; CrackerClips/ iStock/Getty Images Plus; Blackred/E+; T3 Magazine/ Future; GOLFX/iStock/Getty Images Plus; Steve Gorton/Dorling Kindersley; Blackred/E+; Tim Robberts/ The Image Bank; Chain45154/Moment; Stewart Cohen; Beyond fotomedia; Moodboard/Brand X Pictures; SebastianGauert/iStock/Getty Images Plus; Rob Lewine; XiXinXing; **U4**: Dan Bannister/Image Source; Ales-A/ E+; XiXinXing; Ajr_images/iStock/Getty Images Plus; NADOFOTOS/iStock/Getty Images Plus; ajr_images/ iStock/Getty Images Plus; **U5**: Jim Craigmyle/Corbis; Tetra images; Leonello Calvetti/Stocktrek Images; Bettmann; GCShutter/E+; Franckreporter/E+; Matteo Colombo/Moment; Caroline von Tuempling/Photodisc; **U6**: Gail Shotlander/Moment; cinoby/iStock/Getty Images Plus; **U7**: Museimage/Moment; Pgiam/iStock Unreleased; Joe Sohm/Visions of America/Universal Images Group; Paul Marotta; Peter Adams/The Image Bank; TwilightShow/iStock/Getty Images Plus; **U8**: Reza Estakhrian/Photolibrary; Ryan Smith/Corbis; GibsonPictures/E+; Undrey/iStock/Getty Images Plus; Khalid Hawe/UpperCut Images; Ron_Thomas/E+; SDI Productions/E+; **U9**: Hybrid Images/Cultura; Jamie Grill; skynesher/E+; **U10**: Gabriel Perez/Moment; Caiaimage/ Robert Daly; Young Yun/Moment; Hero Images; PeopleImages/E+; **U11**: Ezra Bailey/The Image Bank; Dimedrol68/iStock/Getty Images Plus; Wxin/iStock/ Getty Images Plus; monkeybusinessimages/iStock/ Getty Images Plus; **U12**: DenKuvaiev/iStock/Getty Images Plus; Photo 12/Universal Images Group; Mark Garlick/Science Photo Library; Culture Club/Hulton Archive; Hulton Fine Art Collection; Alfred Eisenstaedt/ The LIFE Picture Collection; Hulton/Archive; Ralph Orlowski/Getty Images Entertainment; Dave J Hogan/ Getty Images Entertainment; **U13**: Marie Meier/ EyeEm; Stefanie Keenan/WireImage; Hindustan Times; Lawrence K. Ho/Los Angeles Times; Jan Cattaneo/ EyeEm; **U14**: Scott Eisen; Gilbert Rondilla Photography/ Moment; John Phillips; Steve Granitz/WireImage; Riccardo Savi; 10'000 Hours/DigitalVision; **U15**: Chris Ryan/OJO Images; Luis Alvarez/DigitalVision.

Illustrations

Ben hasler; Ed Fotheringham; Maria Rabinky; Michael Mantel; Monika Roe; Pat Byrnes; Richard Williams; Rob Schuster.

Audio

Audio production by John Marshall Media

Typeset

Q2A Media Services Pvt. Ltd.